Uncontained Thoughts

Poems by Mark Shoenfield

Published by:

Blue Jade Press, LLC

Blue Jade Press, LLC
Vineland, NJ 08360
www.bluejadepress.com

Special thanks to the Montclair Write Group for their venue and generous time in allowing me to present my work with full acceptance and generous support. Your invisible hand helped make these poems better than first conceived.

To Frances, my partner in life, my moral compass and constant North Star

Table of Contents

Perhaps an Homage to Charles Dickens' (Time)

Late December walk in the forest
gray winter sky
with numbing cold toes

Weeks shy of my seventy-second birthday
never knowing more about life
never knowing less about everything

My vision wider and more acute than ever, while
sometimes missing the obvious right in front of me,
the massive accumulation of knowledge, not always
readily accessible

The comfortable uncomfortable realizations of a long
marriage and the flickering flames of sex turning to
wisps of smoke spiraling outward, friends never more
appreciated and disappointing, two sides of a valuable
coin

Perhaps still attempting to align the inner world with
the outer, the eternal struggle we briefly win every now
and then is the spark that keeps us going, hoping to
reconcile it all, "just as it is"

Sometimes losing the thread of, "this is it", how much
do we reflect and observe wondering if were just
following nature's primordial tracks or following our
own path, in the dense beautiful forest without any trail
markings to guide us but our own desires of free choice

"It was the best of times, it was the worst of times, it was the age of wisdom, it was the age of foolishness, it was the epoch of belief, it was the epoch of incredulity, it was the season of light, it was the season of darkness, it was the spring of hope, it was the winter of despair."

Dickens, C. & Dunn, H. (1921) A Tale of Two Cities. New York, Cosmopolitan Book Corporation. [Image] Retrieved from the Library of Congress, https://www.loc.gov/item/22004431/.

Pandemic 2020

Do the trees know?
Can they sense a distortion of the natural order
as more birds, wildlife and people abound?

Our sailboat of time has slipped from its mooring.
There are no buoys to orient us now.
We once measured our children's growing height
with pencil marks on doors.
Now the days blend together yet the month's sprint by.
The dissonance of standing in place- safe, scared, bored.
Yet the uncelebrated birthdays, anniversaries, hugs and
social gatherings mount in the blurred void of
alienating amnesia.

How can the summer be ending?
I have not worn my bathing suit once.
Yet the weather and seasons yank us forward like an
impatient dog walker with a slumbering pet.

With Zen-like new baby eyes, each new season a virgin
experience, as if never fully felt before.
The leaves will turn dazzling shades, and then scatter.
Cool nighttime breezes will tug bedroom curtains
making sleep a most pleasurable release.
The tile floor will feel cold in the morning.

The seasons, our new old markers of time,
more natural than those we could ever invent
will hold court until man can temporarily outsmart
a virus that has no illusion of time.

Chronicle for New Jersey January 11, 2022

New Jersey, January, 16 degrees, snow on the ground
Morning online meditation class, overall malaise voiced
by the group, of winter, of COVID, of restricted life for
too long, no suitable outlet for frustration, mental
exhaustion, focus on the breath, mind wanders, refocus,
repeat, repeat, repeat

Lunch at café with my wife, masks on masks off, we eat
Are we too foolish? Are we too cautious?
Trip to super market, masks on, we must eat

Afternoon, I go to empty gym
At age seventy what season am I training for?
Aerobic, weights, stretching, why?
My oatmeal breakfasts with blueberries,
My steamed vegetables, brown rice and green tea
lunches, why, to outlive my loved ones and friends?

Evening, we make a fancy dinner, chicken with
couscous, lemon, halloumi cheese and walnuts,
the 2016 Barolo wine with the smooth finish is penning
this tale

Tis the season of boredom, frustration, isolation,
and wine, fueling hope for an inspiration of a good
enough poem for Sunday's online poetry session

Pay It Forward

An acquaintance contacted me to say that she just
purchased three of my previous poetry books for
herself and two friends after reading several of my
poems in a bookstore. I thanked her and voiced my
deep felt appreciation.

I tip three young groundskeepers twenty dollars each
as they trim our hedges today in pouring rain, certain
they are way underpaid by their young, entrepreneurial
boss.

My wife orders a blue hooded bath towel for friend's
new grandson.

We drive to a store, I put on my face mask and
purchase ingredients for a lasagna as my wife waits in
the car. We will eat portions much larger than we
should and drink red wine from Tuscany tonight.

We watched a tear jerking television movie, women's
choral conflict resolved, while their husbands are away
at war, one of them to die.

My wife and I separately sniffle and silently wipe away
a few tears.

A sister-in-law emails to ask if we knew anything about
a new cancer drug being considered for her late stage
cancer patient husband who's running out of options
and time. We email back Internet information we find,
while feeling growing anxiety, panic and helplessness.

We find a local food bank on the internet and donate
money.

A friend is turning seventy next week in this Covid virus age. We will drive past her house and leave a bottle of champagne and a fancy cupcake on her steps to mark the milestone.

My wife and I frequently take long walks yielding distance to folks coming from the opposite direction.

We do what we do, but in our hearts, we know it's not enough.

Sunday morning I retrieve the NY Times from the driveway. I peel back the blue plastic covering to read the headline:

U.S.DEATHS NEAR 100,000, AN INCALCULABLE LOSS

A Drop of Ink

We live in a moderately priced condo development.
Across the way is a Taiwanese Buddhist Conference
building.
Because of ongoing roadwork repair, we were advised
to park our cars behind the Buddhist property.

This past Friday as I prepared to load our car for a
weekend getaway, I was shocked to see hundreds of
cars lined up single file, just waiting.
Waiting for what, I wondered as I loaded our car with
suitcases and golf clubs. I went over to inquire and
learned the cars were on line for food.

Approximately thirty volunteer Asian food pantry
workers of all ages were dispensing boxes of free food
to the waiting cars. Most of the beneficiaries came in
late model cars; some came on foot or bicycle and most
were here by word of mouth.

I call them the invisible poor, and we were ignorant of
their existence, numbers, or proximity to our
community.

My wife and I will be volunteering next Friday
We will do paperwork, or load boxes with food
or put cartons in open car trunks.

I wonder more now, about our agency, actions and family lineage: The triangulating of randomness or choice of the middle class, the Buddhists and the hungry all converging on a summer day in a New Jersey parking lot.

DAE

His name is Dae, D-A-E
He is my working partner at the food pantry
Sixty-four, tall muscular, understated, floppy hat
covering a bald head
A Buddhist non fruit-eating, vegetarian with a strong
mistrust of western medicine
He works tirelessly, selflessly at whatever tasks need to
be done; fork lifting pallets, unloading produce, and
cutting shrink wrapped boxes piled high
Between loading cars with produce we talk, nutrition,
medicine finances cars, life

Raised in Hong Kong the oldest of four siblings
Just seven years old when his father left
for South America to work as a cook
He did not see his father again for ten years
When they then lived in the projects near Trenton New
Jersey, four families sharing a single bathroom
His mother would chase a neighbor's son out of the
bathroom where he regularly shot heroin
Dae was the only Asian in his High School classes
He failed miserably with English but excelled in math
and science

He eventually attended Rutgers College majoring in
Chemical Engineering. He married, had two daughters
who have successful careers in computer science.
Dae's been volunteering every week here at the food
pantry for the last eight years

The American immigrant dream personified,
opportunity, hard work, success
So much many take for granted while knowing so little
about those working right beside us

Buddhist Food Pantry in Winter

February 2, 2023 Northern New Jersey
20 degrees Fahrenheit, gusting winds
Cars line up for a quarter mile waiting

Layered, tee shirt, turtleneck, sweatshirt
scarf, heavy coat, head cover and beanie,
gloves and lined pants
Fingers toes painfully stinging

The legitimately hungry
and the imposters keep coming
bizarrely this week we have mangoes
and watermelons along with the usual fare
of potatoes, onions, eggplant, apples, cabbage, and
cauliflower
Fingers so numb one must pick up entire boxes rather
than using the indented perforated handles

Two hours later when cars reduce to a trickle
some of us jog in circles to try and increase circulation
There is some obtuse pleasure in shared discomfort
this Asian community, loading free food
in cars and trunks, smiling beneath their face masks and
telling the occupants to stay warm
Disregarding the optics of some brand new expensive
cars, and shelving politics for the greater good

Feeling useful and focused, distracted from other
everyday concerns, to be cold, very cold, tired, very
tired and to have done some good for others is a
cleansing experience

This work draws me back week after week
is it penance, gratitude, giving back,
or even worth asking why?

Later a simple meal is provided
a glutinous rice soup with pieces
of potato, mushrooms and tofu that
tastes as good as anything you ever eaten

Next week will be warmer
and the volunteers
and the hungry
will return in the
perpetual cycle

Egg Politics

This week at the food pantry my job was to distribute
boxes of produce and eggs to approximately 250 cars.

The price of eggs has recently more than doubled due
to avian flu, increased cost of feed, packaging and labor.

This was the first time we had eggs to distribute.
I was generally instructed to give one carton per family.

A numerical card placed on each car at check-in
indicates the number of registered families per auto.
As each car pulled up I would pass the egg cartons
through the passenger's side window to a pleasantly
surprised driver or passenger seat occupant.

At first I honored the one carton per family rule.
Occasionally a recipient would ask for an additional
carton and I informed them of the rules.
Later on, with what appeared to be an ample supply of
eggs I would take a more sympathetic attitude, and
after their additional request put a finger to my lips, say
"shush" and give them extra eggs.

This was always acknowledged with great appreciation
Who doesn't like to feel special?
Are we not all a little selfish?

I admit my decision to give extra eggs was selectively
based on who and how they asked.
The more elderly, needy in appearance did influence
me. I enjoyed my latitude in choosing,
"As if I could make fair decisions."

As the afternoon wore on, the egg supply ran out.
I would then tell the drivers about the eggs and ask
them to try and come earlier next week.
Like Halloween, those that come early get the "better
stuff."

I felt bad when one young man said he couldn't
come earlier because he worked. Another was
misinformed about the start time. A woman said
she just finished a chemo treatment and couldn't
arrive any earlier.

How sad so many wait in line so long for eggs and
vegetables in hungry America?
How strange all the factors that determine which
hungry people get eggs to eat today.

(Epilogue- I decided to strictly enforce the one carton per family
rule the following week. However, next week there were no eggs
to be given out.)

The Modern World

Our son is getting married in a few months, maybe a baby within a year. He and his fiancée picked a beautiful upstate winery for their venue.

Today, my wife and I went to see the winery. Perhaps you know the motif, a huge open room, brick walls, exposed rafters, large fireplace, many wine casks, hundreds of wine bottles, a beautiful mahogany bar and wine glasses with the wineries name neatly stenciled on each one. My wife and I are thrilled with their selection. It will be a wonderful affair. We then ate a wonderful, grossly overpriced lunch and left feeling giddy and tipsy from too much afternoon wine.

Tomorrow my wife will put dry goods in 500 brown paper bags. I, along with other Buddhist volunteers, will put over 500 cardboard boxes of produce into all models of cars lined up for at least a quarter of a mile. These cars will have been sitting, waiting over an hour for the free food they cannot afford to buy.

As we walked to our car from the winery, three black military jets suddenly arced across the sky. They were flying low at a forty-five degree angle and their engines pierced the quiet August afternoon. One could not help but think of the current war and loss of life and destruction in Eastern Europe.

We are so happy for friends of ours that are over the moon with the birth of their first grandson.

Another friend was just diagnosed with stage four cancer.

A brother –in- law is going home after three months in the hospital.

Last night I was moved to tears from a television show about family relations.

My wife and I were recently in a store when without any warning or announcement a loud piercing alarm went off. We quickly headed towards the exit while other folks seemingly ignored the warning. I know my wife and I both had the same unspoken thought "active shooter?"

I gratefully put drops in my eyes at night that help preserve my vision.

All random isolated occurrences you might think?

Two of the modern world's most fashionable zeitgeist words of the day are:

Mindfulness-*a mental state achieved by focusing one's awareness on the present moment*) and,

Gratitude- *the quality of being thankful; readiness to show appreciation for and to return kindness.*

Maybe we need more words to help us understand the modern world in which we live in.

Holocaust Museum

Went to a holocaust museum,
doesn't matter which one, they had
old photographs, maps, films, interviews,
uniforms, suit cases, shoes, box cars etc.

Call me naïve, the question is not, "Where was God?"
But where was humanity?

"Remember your hook number" they said
as people disrobed for mandated showers.
I would have believed them when they said
you had to be disinfected before you got new
clothes and a work assignment.

What moved me most, what blurred my eyes with tears
was not the exhibit itself, but seeing the shock, hurt and
pain on the faces of the people who paid admission to
witness the inconceivable as if it were a malignancy
never to metastasize.

Dharma

I'd love to hear a conversation between Freud and
Buddha
Would they sit on a couch in silence, each waiting for
the other to speak?
They pioneered guideposts to the land of less suffering
These twin bookends holding thousands of maps of the
mind, just two "Dharma Bums" "On the Road" to
"Civilization and It's Discontent"

Our minds are designed not to see reality
Our feelings are not reliable
Our attachments cause us pain
Our implied narratives blind us to what truly is
Our hope for permanence a false illusion

Ask the man in the ER thinking he's having a
heart attack when it's only a panic attack?
Ask the gardener the difference between
a flower and a weed?
Ask a Buddhist the difference between
himself and a German?

The closest I have come to enlightenment is when
I chased a baseball, hit from bat to sky attempting with
all my heart to catch it, sprinting with full passion, and
utmost attention as it descended to the ground
It did not matter if I caught it, or the ball plunked to
earth inches from my outstretched hand

I was the ball, the air, and the sky for an eternity

Meditation Number Nine

While preparing to brush my teeth, toothbrush in hand, cold water faucet slowly running, I spied a very small bug, say half the size of a pin head on the counter to my left.

Reflexively, I swiped this defenseless bug into the sink basin. Does such a small living thing possess a central nervous system, can it think, feel pain, have consciousness?

Yet it scurried away from the vortex of clockwise draining water. For a brief second the bug seemed to make headway towards escape but the laws of physics and gravity quickly overruled and down the drain, dare I say, he or she vanished. I prefer not to think of the outcome polymorphism aside.

You the reader are the first to hear my particular take on this occurrence. I'm a little chagrined to dwell on such a momentary slice of mundane life.

Zen Buddhists do not kill insects, it's bad Karma and killing small bugs can be like pennies that can add up to dollars. I live in New Jersey am not a Buddhist and do not often entertain such thoughts. But extinguishing the existence of any living moving thing can cause some degree of deliberation. Should I have rescued said bug and released it somewhere else? Out of sight and out of mind went the bug and this reflection, as it probably will for you as well.

Men's File Cabinet

I think it's fair to say men remember the times
they've declined a woman's sexual favors.

I think it's fair to say women do not remember the
times they rebuffed a man's advances.
There's probably a mathematical equation to explain
this.

I wonder for men, decades or more later, if there lingers
some regret or rationalization?
Maybe there's a sense of towing one's ethical or
judgmental line which fits like a key in a secure lock
that was never violated.

Yet, feeling comfortable with those past decisions,
That is, the "possible" rejection of temptation,
why do I think men stubbornly embed those
recollections?
Is it ego, narcissism, self-righteousness or the history
trail of doubt?
In fact, I might argue, men remember those moments
more so than their conquests.
And "conquest" being such a poor word to choose.
Perhaps it's just the mystery, the story minus the
climax.

A Walk in the Park

Lately after dinner, around dusk, I go for a walk in the
park, though the grass, plants, trees and animals are
alive; stillness pervades the path carved from the larger
dark forest just beyond.

There's a particular bench I often stop by, it overlooks a
green sloping plain, punctuated with scattered trees of
varying grey brown trunks of different heights.
The bench has a plaque "In Loving Memory of Daniel
P. Donovan."

I sit and collect my thoughts pulling in the strings as
they randomly disperse, as if weightless.

Earlier that day, I caught myself utter a word of phrase
that was not mine, but certain it was my deceased older
brother's reincarnation.

We were not close, in fact estranged for years, whether
it's because of genes, his war experiences or just some
distorted perceptions.

He had a sullenness that sometimes resurfaces on my
own son's face, that same reserved look of disgust,
absent of language, that belies the sweet sensitive
wounded pride beneath.

Funny how traits, nuances, moods spiral down through
the generations. Are they real or do we only think we
see them to feel some sense of connection?

My wife and I are much closer these days.
We try harder to out please each other in small ways.
It's a fun game, with no losers.
I make her pancakes on Sundays.
She listens to my poems with full attention.
I print out the daily crossword puzzle for her.
She buys me books on Kindle.
We somehow see, understand the need and benefit of
being the stake that props the other one to stand tall, as
the weight and value of the marriage increases in a way
we, or at least I, never saw before.

I hope our son will find this out much sooner than I did.

I'll let other thoughts of the day escape without
scrutiny. They quickly, gladly, scatter, leaving no
tracks.

I continue my walk around the long circular park's
paths that never fail to reveal something new on each
visit.

A Walk in the Park, Senses On

Sunny, sixty-nine degrees, a scant breeze, a slight chill
or is it warmth in the air? Jacket on or jacket off, one
can't decide as gentle breath envelops bare skin.

The muted hum of cars coming and going, an
unintended backdrop that fades like boredom.

If one keenly concentrates a distant far off bird's chatter
can be heard.

Idle dog walkers talking to their pets as if friends or
humans.

Mothers pushing strollers carrying on one way
conversations with the young ones safely strapped in.

The paved path rolls slightly up and down on black
pebbled asphalt.

The walkway hard and firm underfoot, as socks slide a
bit inside warm rubber soled sneakers.

Can you hear the silence?
Red breasted bird pecking in the grass
other birds follow their leader.
Arthritic finger-like tree limbs
await the signal to burst green buds.

Husband, wife and daughter stroll by and say "Hello."
The warm sun on the back of my neck, just a friendly
reminder of next season's pending arrival. The path
forks, one way to the parking lot, the other for another
loop.

I decide to take Yogi's advice and take the fork, and the sun shines and the pillowy clouds silently pass, and this peaceful part of the earth continues its archetypal design, uninterrupted for now, for all that wish to see, that nothing is static.

A January Walk

A solitary walk in the park
on a cold January day,
bright sunshine clarity
and a gusty biting breeze
stinging my ears

Black, three foot wide
asphalt path littered with
unmelted salt pellets crunching
beneath my feet

Suddenly feeling a pellet
in my shoe between my sock and heel
I step gingerly hoping to continue

Momentarily the pellet slightly shifts
falsely giving me hope of continuing
my journey unabated
toes numbing, eyes watering,
hood strings tightly pulled,
the pellet shifts back again
I realize I must intervene
each step a painful hobbling increment

I find a bench beneath a tree
with twisted leafless branches
Resting my foot for ease, untie my laces,
remove my shoe
and discard a small in size,
large in discomfort, pebble

I try unsuccessfully to retie my laces
with only one gloved hand
then removing my other glove,
stiff fingers in concert finish the tie

I plod on in pleased numbing semi-comfort
Winter rules, the park is empty
the dog walkers, home in front of their fireplaces
the couples, elsewhere in some heated confines

I relish the pain and pleasure of the numbing cold
but do not forget there's value in the offending stone
interrupting my solitude

Drifting Clouds

On a warm July day when I was 12 years old, I lay on my back on the grass in the center of Marine Park smelling the pungent grass that had been cut the day before.

In a large open field glancing towards the horizon, I saw the curvature of the earth in the crease where the earth and sky meet.

Feeling the pull of gravity on my body and a slight dizziness, I stared upward and watched the clouds spreading across the sky.

The clouds constantly changed into new shapes in their perpetual path eastward. The winds of the upper atmosphere pushed the defiant clouds that then reluctantly obeyed with some resistance.

When you concentrate on the clouds you notice how quickly they move. Most people don't give it much thought. They don't have time to watch clouds.

They live their lives and rarely notice, giving but a casual glance skyward and forming a mental shorthand of how the weather might affect them.

Although the park was fairly crowded, children's shouts and ballgame chatter were distant and muffled on the flat open plain far from where I lay.

I remember that day, though it was over 55 years ago
What happened to those clouds?
What happened to that 12 year old boy?

We each swiftly moved across the horizon, forming and
reforming; the changes both slow and swift at the same
time.

I like watching clouds they remind me to pause
and remember there are no pauses
and I too follow the winds of time,
but like the clouds not without some resistance.

Joan

There's a woman in our book club named Joan.
She has been coming for many years.
She is elderly, frail, users a walker,
and is not particularly friendly.

Last month she read the wrong book by mistake.
Joan does not own a computer.
Joan doesn't like books that use profanity.
Her comments are always short and direct.

Last meeting, the back door was locked when it came
time to leave.
Someone asked me to drive Joan's 12 year old Toyota
around to the front.
Scrunched up, I did so without readjusting either the
mirrors or seat.

Joan slowly ambled her way around her car,
folded her walker, with less than stable hands
placing it on the backseat.
She then grabbed the open door for balance
carefully maneuvering herself into the driver's seat.
She thanked me perfunctorily
then slowly drove off, alone into the night.

I'm already looking forward
to seeing Joan next month.

Kate

Other people don't see the two pianos on your back
As you try to walk to the flowery temple for relief
We have lunch
You speak in paragraphs
I speak in sentences
I listen, nod, and give you open seas

You the sage
Caregiver by nature and profession
So careful to bear your burden with
dignity and grace

You play those pianos like Job
Few hear or see the
resonating chords of tears
crescendoing within

Libby

It's not my style to send a "greeting card" to a woman I
hardly know.

Libby had attended our weekly meditation meetings.
She was quiet, soft spoken, engaged, but shy.
The group leader informed us Libby was dying of brain
cancer and would not return.
We were given her address if we wanted to write.

I felt silly selecting a card that read, "Wishing you
peace." So, I wrote, "You will be missed in our group
and you're in our thoughts."

I had no idea what to say to this virtual stranger,
of course the collective group's heart goes out to her.
I suspect, maybe wrongly, that the women in our group
naturally know how to do this much better than I.

What would I want if I were in her place?
I do not know, I cannot imagine.

Perhaps these small acts of kindness make us all feel
a little more connected, and maybe that's all we can do,
to see, to recognize each other and silently knowingly
nod.

*We were told by LB's cousins that she was thrilled and deeply
touched to receive so many cards. She planned to thank everyone on
zoom but was too tired to do so.*

Paul

When the egg is fertilized by the sperm, is when you
obtain the death warrant. Knowing about extinction,
but not the exact date, is supposed to make life
valuable. This is what makes relationships precious.

How trite to say we don't use our time expeditiously.
How, to reconcile with those that won't?
How, to get others to see the errors of their ways?
How, to accept others that act against their own best
interests?
How, to hold a grudge, a hurt, for a lifetime?
How, not to see the larger picture?
How, to take these things to your grave?

I know many do.

I do not understand those that fail to forgive errors of
youth.
I do not understand those that reject love.
I do not understand death, the final No!

There are no winners, only losers.
Perhaps this makes you silent, reflective,
uneasy, angry, sad?

That's what the living are left with, just memories,
regrets, and what ifs and why not's?

Such a heavy load to tote forever.

Paulette

She said her name was Paulette, that first day at work, attentive, engaged but somehow distant and mysterious. She was well dressed, attractive, with an angular nose that made for an unusual look, but did not detract in the least.

Work makes "strange bedfellows" as they say, and yet I felt an undefined affinity, her pull, like a magnet attracting metal filings.

Once the company van took us to a scenic outing for a conference. After, Paulette and I walked by a murky lake, she said she felt a strong desire to swim but it would shock her co-workers and also she didn't want to wear wet under clothes going home. Then as if talking to herself she said her "ex-husband always had difficulty unclasping her bra."

The pieces of her puzzle had sharp edges that didn't fit together well.

Then one day at a team meeting, she suddenly stood and announced said she was leaving the company. She thanked everyone and made a point of touching each of us, on the arm or shoulder and walked out the same way she walked in six months prior.

The human brain can speculate a thousand wrong reasons for someone's motives. But we're just left with the fact that Paulette chose to remain a mystery.
I sent her an email, and no reply came.

Unlike metal filings left on the table when a magnet is removed, people are always left wondering why some attractions end.

An Elementary School Mate

A sports celebrity died yesterday.
I read his long obituary in the New York Times.
We were school mates sixty years ago, at PS 194,
that played punch ball on a Brooklyn cement
schoolyard. I followed his career from a distance, never
speaking to him past the sixth grade.

He died at age seventy, my current age.

Memories, the indelible fingerprints that span decades.
He looked out for, like an older brother, a severely
challenged student in our class, I did not know why?
His love of the sport demonstrated in a third grade
show and tell presentation. We frustrated our teacher
Mrs. Bookman chasing errant pink rubber balls gone
astray into the street, as if life or death depended on it.

I cheer his accomplishments, his glory, and his fame. I
mourn his death, our youth, the inevitable passing of
time.

We are human, we can hold more than one feeling in
our heart at the same time.

Who can I tell? Who would understand? These ineffable
feelings will live as long as I do encased in a
melancholy sentimental aging mind.

Dissonance

My brother in-law John is dying of cancer.
He called this morning from Florida to speak to his
sister, my wife. He sounded as if he were in the room
next door. He sounded good, too good to be dying.
His anti-cancer medication has stopped working.
We talk and try to sound mature, the underground
river of fear silently snaking its way to the sea.
He and his wife moved down there a year ago, away
from family and friends. Made no sense to us, but
people do what they do.

I was thinking about John while showering this
morning. After stepping out of the stall, as I began
shaving, a familiar happy catchy upbeat love song came
on the radio. It was like two disharmonious or
unsuitable elements colliding as they often do in life.

My wife and I walked a mile and a half to the
supermarket this afternoon. It was one of those cool
crisp bright calm, blue skied spring March days,
pink and orange red buds swelling from bent finger
branches timing their blooms with anticipation.

Walking home with groceries evenly distributed,
fragments of a poem started to come together, thoughts,
ideas, rhythm. Yet when we arrived home the essence
of the poem had dissipated. Evaporated like a road
mirage approached on a hot day.

My wife and I seldom eat red meat; you know fat,
cholesterol, nitrates. Tonight we will eat hot dogs and
silently think of John.

Baseball Dream

On a February winter morning at 4:12 am
I suddenly awake from a dream
feeling supreme confidence and joy
the dream, of being eighteen years old
in the athletic bloom of life
with purpose and identity unquestionably defined

Awaiting my turn in batting practice
I patiently watch the coach soft toss scuffed baseballs
as the hitter in the cage, dribbles soft grounders, meager
popups and humpback liners around the diamond

The field littered with balls in various stages of wear
like popcorn scattered on a green and brown backdrop
some glossy white with bright red stitching
others scuffed with brown baked in dirt

I grab my 34 ounce bottle necked Nellie Fox bat
the one I once hit four shoulder high meatballs over a
310 foot sign causing a birddog scout, pen and index
card in hand to come chat me up

I'm supremely confident that the marriage
of mind and body will rip
the first batting practice pitch on a tight rope down the
right field line
with a distinct crack that will turn heads

At age seventy-one, I play all the positions on this
gestalt diamond team

I am the youth
I am the first feeble hitter
I am the confident slugger
I am the older coach
I am the new glossy baseball
I am the older scuffed worn ball

Today my uniform hangs in the closet
how remarkable, the memory synapses
more than fifty years later,
retain the indelible wish to play

Double Play

Forty-two years old
Sitting in the backseat of a car driving through Brooklyn
A coach is talking to me but I'm not listening

Do I want to play next season?
Roam the green plains of centerfield again?
Snaring blurred white liners hit in the gap?
Deflating the dreams of hitters,
collecting nods of approval from my
manager and teammates pats on my back

Knowing now I can't cover the ground
Knowing now my legs will fail me
Knowing now my arm strength is gone

I want to play
I want my prowess back
Youth exhausted, spent at forty-two

Maybe my wife stirs beside me?
Maybe a noise from outside?
Like the roar of the crowd at the crack of the bat
I'm summoned to immediate confused consciousness
To awaken, shaken, in the dark
at age seventy two is quite the double play

42 Middle age
42 Willie May's age when he retired
42 Jackie Robinson's number

Late Innings

A pitcher who's lost his fastball late in the game
isn't removed from the fracas
Pride, ego, and standing battered if he tries
his once favored pitch
Shame, the residue on the scoreboard
for all the world to see

Adjust, adapt, and see the world differently
throw off speed junk, knuckleballs, hugs and kisses?

Act as if you don't care, pretend, play the jester
But give up the game, how?

Retreat into silence
a hollow cardboard shield,
wholly insignificant to ward off the blows

Join the aged masses in bitter surrender
You had your glory
Accept the game as an observer

You try and ignore the crowd's roar
as you loiter, linger outside the
high thick stadium walls
wondering what's happening inside,
as imagination clings to hope

Nostalgically knowing better,
that only sweet memories remain

Boxing Class

My friend coaxed me into attending a boxing class at
the local Y. Almost sixty-eight at the time and not
having thrown a punch in anger in over five decades:

I harbor no inward aggression
I do not seethe at the world
I do not wish to punish/dominate anyone physically
I attend out of curiosity and the need for exercise

The early morning class consists of ten participants,
surprisingly eight women and my friend and I. The
instructor tutors us in how to hit the "heavy bag" that is
suspended from the ceiling and is anchored to the floor.
A taut solid black cylinder that sways slightly with each
punch.

How stimulating is it to punch a bag, over and over?
Well it turns out there's quite a bit to know, stance,
balance, speed, technical mechanics, a physical chess
match of mind and body.

Muscle memory to be practiced over and over, as if
assembling a toaster part by part, faster and faster, not
very intuitive to the uninitiated.

One could say the intent is to learn to hurt someone if
the need arises, or more diplomatically, how to defend
oneself if assaulted. I suppose that is why the
preponderance of women in the class.

Zen like concentration, punching, puts you in the here
and now, as one goes inward, burrowing into some
unexplored channel of ancestral violence.

Boxing an individual act, practiced in a group setting.
Jab jab hook, pop pop boom, pop pop boom, pop pop
boom pop pop boom poppopboom
Faster and faster the instructor implores in specific
timed intervals.

"Stop!" he finally shouts, my erratic rhythm halted on a
dime. Bent over, hands on knees, sucking wind my
body sweating profusely, rest very welcomed.

I know tonight, tomorrow, my hands, wrists and
shoulders will ache. But I will be back next week.

*I wish to learn more about the physical translation between my
brain and body, to get them in a coordinated dance step that
seamlessly compliments one another.*

Father Time
(24, 9, 15, 27, 31, Uniform Numbers)

As a boy I idolized my favorite sports heroes.
I lived and died with each exploit, thrilled and
exulted by their amazing athletic achievements,
660 home runs, 50 goals, great catches, championships.

I copied their style, swagger, and was captivated by
their public adulation. I, like many boys of a certain age,
hoped one day to be a star athlete. Many of my early
idols are now dead or in their eighties or nineties,
some with quite unpleasant pasts newly revealed.

I'm currently reading a new biography about one
former hero, now reassessed through the lens of time. It
casts an autumn shadow back on his youthful life and
exploits.

How will I feel when someday soon this legend has
passed? A few news cycles of old highlights, the same
film clips will be played over and over. Elderly
gentlemen and former teammates will speak laudatory
comments.

There's a photo on my desk in our den, it shows my
wife, son and I atop New Hampshire's Mount
Washington. We're all smiling, with our arms around
each other; at my current age I probably will never
climb that mountain again.

When I was younger I played basketball on hot humid
August nights in Brooklyn. I was so limber I could palm
the cement pavement with straight knees. Now I use a
tree shoe horn when getting dressed in the morning.

I knew an eighty-six year old man, who refused an operation that would extend his life. He declined, and wished to let nature take its course. He was world weary, but I could not understand his decision. Maybe you're only supposed to see so much, in this life?

Some wisdom is parceled out slowly, like attending a long afternoon double header that begins in bright sunshine and gives way to darkening night skies.

These are some thoughts you have when you have outlived your father by twenty years and your boyhood idols are filling the cemeteries.

The Lingering Heart

My mother died in 2016, suddenly, if you can say such a thing at age 92. We received a frantic call from the assisted living facility where she had resided. I said my private goodbyes waiting for the funeral home people to arrive. I stood before her peaceful body in that quiet surreal room, and three times I left that room and three times I returned. The lingering heart does not release easily.

My father died in 1973 at age 52. He had worked in a brownstone on a residential street in Greenwich.

Last weekend my wife and I drove from suburban NJ into Manhattan for a day of people watching and sight-seeing as we're wont to do. We found ourselves just a few blocks from that brownstone and were drawn as if by invisible tugging cords to that building. I stood outside, my hands on the gate, certain my father had touched the same cold iron almost fifty years ago, and that he stood on the same pavement now below my feet.

After a few moments my wife said "let's go" nervous that the current tenants would wonder who was staring into their window? I lingered as long as I could, not wanting to let go of that railing.

And Now

Oh mother you weren't there, when you were there
Oh father you weren't there, when you were there
Oh brother you weren't there, when you were there

Lost I am now to wander here and there in the
wilderness searching for a decipherable path
Not surprisingly I can't find my way home
I can see enough to be blind
I can hear enough to be deaf
I am crippled enough to yearn

Do I stare too long into the reflective pool
as the elusive rainbow is always over there?
Limping on the narrowing train tracks seeking
billboard distractions to idle away the time
Drag others, lead others and follow others on the
roundabout to nowhere
Am I wasting time, should I stare toward or away from
the abyss?

Were my mother, father, older brother lost souls
wandering in their own personal desert searching for
Eden among strangers, running from their own, like
shooting stars in the cold universe?
What is left to learn from their faded starbursts of
smoke and darkness?

It's like the only running movie in a lonely town with
an audience of one, played over and over until the
lights come up revealing an empty theater

Seal the Deal

Once upon a time I had a real estate license.
There were training classes, and an instructor who
taught us how to parry any comment by either the
buyer or seller, a logical "how to" return lob to disarm
any question or statement that might deter or obstruct a
possible sale. I was amazed at the skill and deceit of
such tactics.

One day when I was ten or twelve years old my father
was loading the car. His arms were filled, and he was
angry at me for some irritation.

He tried to kick me!
His forceful attempt missed by inches.
Sixty years later I feel the pain as if his kick had landed.

What could I have done to provoke such ire?
He was not a violent man.
I was not a rebellious kid.
What was the truth of that day?

I'm sure the real estate instructor could provide
a great response for either my father or me.

As if a single truth exists,
or we just pad our feelings
with skillful deceitful language
to seal the deal
and hope in the aftermath
there's neither any
buyers' or sellers' remorse.

Unfinished Business

Sometimes In the early morning around dawn
the pool of memories under the surface glimmers for a
moment and lets you bathe in the water before receding
almost like a mirage disappearing in the mid-day sun as
your approach

You gave us your embers that warmed from a distance,
but kept your roaring fire that nurtured and consumed
you
Were we not worthy?
Left us a lifetime void to ponder the question

You were cool, it was the 1960's
You tried on all the roles of the day
You had your Meerschaum pipe, your goatee,
and Leonard Cohen and Richie Havens records
one step ahead of the societal hipsters you sprinted
The yearning search for answers out there when you
should have used that shrewd intelligence to look
within

You ran from us
out of what, boredom, fear, temptation, curiosity?
The infantile need of I want, versus the adult guide rails
of knowing the consequences
You plunged over the side thinking you could navigate
the road
You were wrong

Time ran out before adequately blending your two
desires but the damage had been done

How sad to be seventy and yell at your dead father in a dream "You weren't there for me" and his silent face unable to reply, my unconscious mind unable to concoct a response

That's what we summarize and call a life lived, and two generations, one gone, the other left with unanswered questions

Hemingway's Collateral Damage

My father, in 1960, unshaven, torn tee shirt, sugar cane
in hand, grinning, thought himself the returning
adventurer at JFK airport as he waved to us
through the glass partition

My father drove the family from Brooklyn New York to
Mexico City in the summer of 1965 in an unair-
conditioned car, to see bullfights

My father, in 1969, made me get him a takeout martini
when he was in the hospital recovering from his second
heart attack

My father bought a small sailboat to feel like a sailor

My father tried to bring home a pretty young woman
from Sweden to stay with us in my mother's house

My father declined a position in Haiti to write
government propaganda for Papa Doc Duvalier

My parents divorced in 1969, father living with a new
woman on Manhattan's Upper West Side

My father
the failed husband
the failed father
the failed writer
thought he could juggle it all
misjudging the emotional cost of stoking his narcissism

My father was not Hemmingway
(who died July 2, 1961 at age sixty-one)
My father died July 2, 1973 at age fifty-two

His wake still ripples- "He went out too far"

The real adventure was right here in front of him
and he missed it

I Met the Happiest Person in the World Today

Her emotions float on the whitest of puffy clouds
She gently takes your hand leading into her special
realm
Her playfulness bubbles over in earnest regard
The openhearted smile as precious as any gemstone

Your comfort and concerns are well considered in her
joyful world
Her games are simple; you race around in an insulated
bubble of delight
She easily laughs from the depths of her core
with a spontaneity that vividly sparkles your universe

Oh the sweet joy of a happy well loved
four-year old, that brings such bliss to the world

So much we have forgotten, so much we can relearn
(As the scars of time have yet to blemish the psyche)
of one so pure, sweet Carra

Floccinaucinihilipilification

(Noun: the action or habit of estimating something as worthless)

How many poems have we read that qualify as
floccinaucinihilipilification?

Possibly being apocryphal or turbid
that do not read like zephyrs but obdurate
as they attempt to munificent exigency
but really are mendacious and the opposite of
pellucidity

Self-interlocutors attempting to evince say,
pulchritude's but alienating the reader's mind to
frustration and indifference

So the reader turns on the radio and hears by chance
"Bridge Over Troubled Water"
she welcomes home the simplicity of soaring music,
harmonized melody and the simple pleasure and
emotion of everyday language

The listener rejoices in the warming bosom of mass
culture connected and contented,
as she joyfully sings aloud and off key

The Herd

I hang around the outskirts of Montclair with the old
grey elephants now.

We attend lectures, movies, and discussion groups
together.
It's a voluntary membership that allows you to join the
herd, being of a certain age and retired are the crucial
requirements.

I watch and learn walking in their huge footprints on
the cement savannas of suburban New Jersey.

I like to watch when they pick up a scent as if I can
somehow glean an important piece of information that
will serve me later.

I'd like to think I'm a little sprier, more nimble, and able
to avoid the relentless lions waiting to ambush the slow
moving pachyderms.

Sometimes the lions attack in packs and drag the
elephant down quickly. Sometimes it's just one lion
slowly following for years, just a bite at a time.

The wrinkled elephants move slowly.
They don't get too excited.
They've been around the block a few times.
They know the true lay of the land.
They avoid peanuts and prefer vegetarian restaurants.

Sometimes they ask the waiter's to wrap up their half-
eaten early bird dinners to have for lunch the next day.

They don't like to drive at night, cloudy eyes, and slower reflexes cause my friends to bump into more trees and misstep in the bush.

They have gathered pretty much all the wisdom they need. It's the simple pleasures that are cherished now, a walk in the park, the warm sun on the mud crusted cheeks, and a long cool drink of noncarbonated water.

They know the law of the jungle and keep their eyes peeled as they trudge to the next watering hole or new restaurant that has a lunch special.

Beware the Deeply Discounted Watermelon

As I entered the supermarket I saw a large bin of ripe watermelons. There were fifty or so oval, round, green striped, heavy watermelons with yellowish white under bellies.

The sign above read, SALE $7.99 (three dollars off) I thumped a few until I found one of my liking and proceeded to the checkout counter. While in line, a kind store employee informed me the sale was only good if you spend an additional ten dollars.

Annoyed but still in the game, I grabbed a bottle of olive oil and bananas, and confidently returned once again to the checkout counter. When the plastic bar coded key tag failed to register the discount, I was befuddled and sought help. I was told I needed the digital coupon for such discount, and should register my personal information at the store kiosk.

In for a penny in for a pound. Patiently a store employee walked me over to the kiosk (that I had never before observed in my twelve years of shopping there) and instructed me how to get the digital coupon added to my coded key tag. The employee then proceeded to fill out various forms and informed me my discount would take a few days to process but would still be valid today.

I left feeling vindicated. I came for a $7.99 watermelon and I left with a $7.99 watermelon; albeit twenty-five minutes later (with unneeded olive oil and bananas in tow).

Two days later, feeling sophisticated and confident
I returned to said store to purchase yet another
watermelon (for a friend's outdoor gathering).

With self-assurance I strode directly to the store kiosk
to demonstrate my newly learned digital coupon skills.
I signed in, entered watermelon in the search field, and
nothing came up. I tried unsuccessful variations of the
search method, nada, zippo nothing "No search results
found."

Feeling angry, foolish and annoyed I sought help.
I was then informed "only one discounted watermelon
per customer."

This is why we need strong gun control laws to prevent
murder and or suicide.

Befuddled to Eureka

My wife and I bought a new glass kitchen table.
It came from China.
It arrived only 10 days after we ordered it.

The rectangular box weighed seventy-five pounds.
I dragged it into the kitchen and we removed all the
contents.

Instruction sheet, chrome legs, railings and glass, no
screws, washers or Allen wrenches could be found
anywhere.

Befuddled, my wife said, "Look in the cardboard box
again, the one I had just discarded."
Eureka, we find a small package of hardware taped to
the bottom of the box.

How difficult is it for two adults to assemble four legs
to a frame and add a glass top, using just 12 screws,
four washers and two Allen wrenches?

The pictured instructions seemed simple enough but,
there was no 800 phone number if problems arose.

I scraped the screws across a bar of soap for easier
piloting and assembled the four legs to the railings
using the appropriate Allen wrench.
Laying the glass top in place we discovered, it was
three inches too long!

Befuddled again, we loosened the screws to expand the
railings, but the glass still extended beyond the
margins.

Baffled and annoyed, should we try calling the company, have the glass cut, or return the whole table to the store?

My wife suggests, we remove all the screws and reverse the legs from inside the railings to outside.

We follow her suggestion, retightened the screws, and eureka the glass top fit perfectly!

I sadly think of my friend Linda, who recently lost her husband of fifty years.
She told me it's so hard having no one to help her change a befuddled moment to eureka!

To assemble a good life together without an 800 number for help, and figure it out together does not go unnoticed.

Gold Coins of the World

On a cold dreary January day my wife and I went to an
upscale market, we wanted to buy delicious chocolate
almond flour cookies.

Forty dollars later with a wagon half full of unnecessary
comfort foods we arrived at the cashier stand.

Nearby, an eye level display featured gold foiled
covered chocolate "Coins of the World" in mesh bags,
I asked my wife if she was tempted.

She nodded no, so I asked the cashier, a short woman of
undetermined age if she indeed wanted a bag of gold
coins.

She quizzically looked at me and declined.
I said, "Who doesn't want a bag of gold coins?"
she declined again, and scanned and bagged our items.

As we prepared to leave, she open heartily smiled, and
offered us the coins for free, I said we were trying to
lose weight and politely declined.

I suggested she share the coins with her fellow workers
She nodded yes, and my wife joining the fun said, "We
will even pay for them."
And the sweet chocolate coins of the world were
distributed to smiling strangers.

How simple life can be, a coin, a gesture, a smile,
whose day was judged the brighter.

A Fall in the Street

My wife tripped and fell in the street
Blood flowed from above her eyebrow
Blood stained her torn jeans at the knee
One moment, one slip, not like childhood

Nauseous, she waited on the sidewalk
Sweat forming beneath my scarf as I hurried to our
parked car blocks away

We drove to an "Urgent Care Center," closed
We drove to a second "Urgent Care Center"
A blood soaked handkerchief pressed above her eye
They refused to see her, "We don't treat head wounds"
Next we went to a pharmacy "Walk in clinic"
Their computer check-in kiosk was broken
I cornered a doctor, who kindly said to "Go to the ER"

Hospital ER parking lot filled to capacity
We wait in triage waiting line
Escorted to an empty room
Assistant comes in, records personal information
We are told to wait

Physician assistant comes in, does cursory assessment
We are told to wait
Doctor comes in, cleans the ugly laceration,
sends my wife for CT head scan
We wait some more

Doctor returns, luckily, scan is negative
He "glues" the wound shut and orders antibiotics
Physician assistant returns, gives tetanus shot, wife
signs more papers
We are allowed to leave

One trip, fall, and the dominoes tumble,
a pleasant early March morning walk transformed
(luckily) into nothing more than an inconvenient scare
but indelible scars will remain

It's An Old Story

Perhaps you know it?
Years ago my wife and I bought an accent chair for the
living room. It was a wingback chair of moderate cost,
with blue and white stripes.

She believed it should be positioned near our wooden
cocktail table. I believed it should be placed further
back near an alcove.

We argued for years about the proper placement of the
chair. The reasons don't really matter.
What was aesthetically pleasing to my wife was quite
irritating to me. Each and every time I entered the
room an inward sigh upped by one the tally of my
nonverbal annoyance.

And yet years later, after my wife passed away
I could not bring myself to reposition the chair.
The desire to subtract the irritation was no longer
present.
Was it guilt, contrition, homage?
How fickle, and childish, and deep, love is.
I told you it's an old story.

House of Straw

A man and a woman meet and go on a date.

Over time the relationship is cobbled together
with brick and lust.
Over time he reveals his business plan.
Over time she silently signs the papers.
The deal is sealed.
The marriage begins with unspoken agreements.
Acquiescence to let the man lead.
Acquiescence to let the man call the shots.
Acquiescence for the woman to follow.

Over time the woman grows resentful.
Over time she wants to modify the plan.
Over time she doesn't want what she once wanted.

The man is confused.
He has gotten his way for so long.
He does not see or sense the gathering wind,
the gale that scatters the straw,
that once was brick and lust
all over their now barren harvested field.

Just a Wager?

Place a bet
The largest wager of your life, marriage
A Las Vegas one armed bandit gambit
Head, heart, sex, devotion, forever
Pull the lever
Watch the tumblers spin,
Ding ding ding
Is there a winner?
Is the game rigged?
If you lose is your wallet thick enough for another spin?
If you win, can you stand up and walk away content?
Notice, no clocks on the walls and free drinks
How compelling the temptations?
Or is it the action you crave to pass the time
the adrenaline rush
till the real game is over

The Mirror's Reflection

Marriage can seem like a never ending arm wrestling
match. Do we enjoy the competition, the heart to heart
combat? Do we really want to win, punish, or absolve
some hidden guilt?

A spouse holds up a mirror reflecting our hurtful
behavior. It's easier to get angry at the mirror holder or
the reflection rather than the stark image we painfully
want to disavow ownership of

How old is this image, how sharply in focus?
Is it recognizable, hazily reminiscent like the self-
discovery of leafing through old family photo albums?

If we cannot alter this reflection and the constant
drawing attention to these faults becomes intolerable to
our spouse or to ourselves then what?

Do not couples fight over the same issues year after
year? At what grave cost to keep changing the mirror
holder?

It's like running in place, going nowhere while the
existential clock keeps ticking down; and the day is
coming when the mirror or the viewer will be covered
with a sheet

Ah, the simple answer you anxiously shout
"Just change your behavior fool
Stop behaving that way
Think before you act"

You pitifully reply
"Have you ever tried to change your reflection?
I can wear sun glasses and a hat, style my hair in a
different manner, lose ten pounds but you could pick
me out of any lineup"

So with attempted mindfulness you guard against
yourself, and sneak peeks at your spouse to see if the
reflection is softening

For one never loses their shadow it only grows longer
or shorter

The Left Handed Proposal

The young couple had been dating for a year.
They were well suited for each other.
They were to meet up at their favorite restaurant for
dinner at seven.
She was on time.
He was late.

He walked in and saw her talking to a stranger.
The stranger was a player, handsome, and
well-dressed with a mischievous smile.

She was taken with his allure.
The stranger was a magnet.
She was just another shiny tin can.

She was over her head.
She was out of her league.
She liked the danger out on the tightrope.
She was losing her balance.

The boyfriend was angry.
The boyfriend was hurt.
The boyfriend saw his future slipping away.
The boyfriend confronted her.

The boyfriend shouted.
The girlfriend cried.
The boyfriend yelled.

"You want to spend the night with him or a lifetime
with me?"

Several years later with two young children sleeping securely upstairs and the couple sipping wine downstairs by the fire in the den, the husband replayed the long ago scene.

The wife had been tempted by a pawn.
She had planned only one move ahead.
The husband risked his queen.
He had seen the whole board and won the game for both of them.

Tire Valve Cap

My wife and I were leaving early Sunday morning on a
car trip. The night before as I exited a restaurant with
our take out order, I noticed the one tire had an exposed
valve, bronze in color, threaded, naked, it caught the
glint of the fading sun.

How had its black cap disappeared?
Had a teenager absconded with it?
Was the cap defective?
Had simply road vibrations dislodged it?

My impulse was surprise and annoyance.
The other three tire caps had never vanished.
How bad can driving without the valve cap be?
I wanted the ten cent piece of plastic back ASAP!

How hard to swipe a cap from the car next to me?
Who would know? It's not exactly grand larceny
Maybe that's how mine wound up missing?

Returning home I parked in an underground garage.
So strong my desire, to remove the cap from the car
parked alongside mine, kneeling down who would see?
What are the odds of being found out?

Sunday, hundreds of miles from home I entered a
hardware store. I told the owner my story.
He frowned when I told him I coveted a stranger's
valve cap. He smiled when I told him I had borrowed
one from my wife's car instead.

He was glad nevertheless when I bought four new valve caps for glove box storage. Maybe I buoyed his faith in man. How thin the line between right and wrong, desire and action.

Jury Duty

I am one of three hundred jurors summoned for a single case.

We watch two films and one PowerPoint presentation, instructing us of our duties and the workings of the court system.
We are given handouts with some of the following numbered questions:

1. Do you understand the defendant is considered innocent until proven guilty?
2. Can you acquit if the prosecution fails to prove its case?
3. Do you understand the defendant does not have to testify?
4. Do you think the justice system is fair?
5. Do you think police tell the truth?
6. Do you think there's some guilt implied just by being a defendant?
7. Do you think you can be a fair and impartial juror?

Many of us think we can be fair jurors.

The burly defendant with head cast down is sitting at a table with his sole attorney.
Two well-dressed prosecutors sit nearby silently scribbling notes.
The judge explains the case.
The defendant is accused of raping his three daughters.

We are told we all have biases.
We are told to honestly answer the numbered questions
Yes or No.

I wonder how many answer truthfully.
I wonder how many wish to avoid serving.
I wonder when it went from the theoretical
to the practical how many recognized
their true face in the mirror?
I wonder how many are ashamed.
I wonder how many feel righteous.
I'll never know.

I cannot say more.
I was dismissed from the case.

Micro Benevolence

We both had shopping carts
filled with non-descript items
We randomly converged
at the end of an aisle
Clearly, neither had right of way

Momentary stalemate,
"You go"
"No you go,"
"No you go"

Two shoppers at right angles
A man, a woman
One black, one white
One older one younger
Both willing to cede ground to the other

With a smile and a small wave of my hand
I said again "you go"
Smiling back, came a soft reply of "thank you"
and we passed by each other momentarily
making significant eye contact

This was more than politeness
more than good manners
more than the social contract

Something in the smile, voice
demeanor said so much more
than our words conveyed

We transcended kindness
or maybe I just wanted to think so

Each of us now a little better off
The memory lingers in my mind
So I retell the story to you

These are the little moments
that illuminate our lives
and give us hope

The Tease

April, May, with their tease days
Put the flannel shirts to the left in the closet
These select balmy days with the powerful allure that
drives you outside acknowledging another quarter turn
of earthly axis

Remembering early morning bus rides past Marine
Park along Avenue R to the train station for another
work day, luscious sunlight streaming in the bus
window, the unnecessary light jacket left at home
A gnawing of the soul, the strong desire to be free
and do something, anything outdoors

Six decades ago, remembering early morning baseball
practices
The sound of batted balls echoing off the apartment
buildings behind us on Caton Ave in springtime
Brooklyn
The dew making white mush baseballs from rolling in
the outfield grass
The balls then to slippery to accurately grasp and throw

Today so powerful the urge to open the windows, walk
in the park, feel the delicate breeze on now uncovered
winter skin, resisting going inside, searching for how to
fully experience the tease, the bait, the delight of spring

And yet, so and so is looking for a cancer clinical trial
And yet, so and so lost her husband six months ago
And age spots have not so magically appeared on my
hands, and the profile I see reflected in a three-way
mirror is somehow a stranger to me

I cast my eyes forward, with gratitude, but can't help steal a glance over my shoulder, to see a shadow while still enjoying the delicate warmth of this day's sun

The Old Man with a Scowl Sitting on the Bar Stool

Perhaps you have seen him, the old man who could not place the value of a relationship over his individual needs.

The chisel of time trimmed away his compliance to compromise leaving a bitter taste of the world in his hungry mouth. He gruffly spits here and there, holding a false sense of self-righteousness, almost slamming shut the door on introspection, but loneliness and doubt had wedged themselves between the jamb and saddle.

The sliver of light that entered was too blinding and painful to illuminate what needed to be seen. He sits mundanely alone at bars or outdoor cafes with maybe a lit cigarette and a wisp of smoke spiraling up into the ether. He walked away from intimacy, as the cost was more than his emotional billfold could afford.

No one was going to run his life or frivolously waste his time.

He slowly watches the sands of time being dredged away, never understanding that he had the power to sculpt a precious sand castle in that wasted wink of an eye that is all the time we have.

Stop Light

I stop for a red traffic light, and glance out the
passenger window. A father, mother, and their boy sit
at an outdoor ice cream parlor. The boy, head down is
absorbed eating his melting ice-cream.

He holds his spoon in a tight fist.
The mother's face is buried in her iPhone.
The father is sitting with legs crossed, a bored
vacant look in his eyes.

I doubt any of them will remember this moment a day,
a week, a month from now, but they may wish for a
second chance decades from now.

How I wish the father would lean over and kiss his boy
on the forehead or tousle his hair. How I wish the
mother would look up, smile or touch her husband's
arm.

The traffic light turns green. I drive off, left to ponder
this frozen moment. I sneak a last glimpse in the rear
view mirror attempting one more hopeful look back.

Snap Shot at the Pool

I know a ninety year old recent widower named Tom.
He looks seventy and likes to ask a lot of questions.
Tom comes to the swimming pool nearly every day.
Today he wore a bright yellow swim suit. He signs in
and looks for someone to talk to. Last week he asked
me if I watch baseball games in the evening.

Today as he was leaving, he side glanced a bunch of
elderly women, six or seven white haired ladies sitting
in a semi-circle. They seemed to give no notice to Tom,
or really each other. They were all talking at once, with
not one seeming to listen. Each lady was speaking
louder over the others as if to command attention.

At the table with the sign-out sheet, Tom lingered
preparing to leave. He paused a bit too long before
opening the gate and with his head down he slowly
trudged off.

The River

Standing on the Little Falls River bank
a floral view framed by yawning green trees
forms a window view across a rolling torrent

The flowing river, like life itself,
unable to see either the beginning or the end
caught in the immediacy of its drag

How swift the current
my seventy years swept along
in a moment, and an eternity

I see the muddy eddy's swirling,
pulled towards the falls
the roar and mist rising
as the river drops down over stationary
sentry boulders, crashing and spraying
on its run to aimless antiquity

I turn to leave the river
as if turning my back
can halt the flow of time

Moving

Remember when you were a kid, sitting in the back seat
of your parent's car with a friend and your parents
started arguing about something. You thought you
would die of embarrassment.

Well, my wife and I argue like that now, with no one in
the back seat.

We're simultaneously selling our home and buying a
condo. Hey, we're adults, we have moved before, we
should be able to control our emotions. But we can't.

We yell at each other, we snipe, we fume and we make
illogical arguments about:
the negotiations,
the appraisals,
the inspections,
the surveys,
the oil tank sweep,
the lawyers,
the paperwork,
the movers,
the phone calls,
the dependence on each other,
the packing,
the hurry up and wait,
the insomnia,
the thousand decisions and actions to make and take,
the stress

We both want and believe this is the right excitable
decision.

Clean out the attic, the garage, keep or throw away,
books, clothes furniture, and our son's lifetime
milestones, mementos etc. We know these are just
"things."

We both know this could be our last move together,
a last stand, our Alamo. A change for the good that
draws forth a primitive fear. The symbolic and literal
leaving home, the unconscious familiar security
traded for the unconscious unfamiliar.

Because really isn't a kitchen just a kitchen, a living
room a living room? Why doesn't logic tamp down the
primitive impulses? The unseen primitive monster so
much scarier than reality, but...

It will all most likely work out for the best, knowing
this is the fuel to proceed. Yet anxiety lurks like a
marionettes' manipulating the puppet's strings.
I cannot do this calmly, rationally; this is the price I
must pay for something I want. I freely confess to you
the reader.

What can you say to assuage my fears?
Some of you will laugh, or commiserate, or perhaps
think me immature, but it's the internal struggle of
welcoming change and fearing it at the same time. It
pits the conscious verse the unconscious in a titanic
struggle.

As Willie Loman's wife stated repeatedly- "Attention
must be paid." Everything has a price.

"Hey honey, where are those change of address cards
again?"

More than Mere Brushstrokes

Painting, covering up the past and present creating a
new future in real time. How many more rooms can, or
will I paint in the future?

My friends and peers are already handing off the chore
to paid assistants. The arthritis, ladder climbing,
messiness no longer seems worth the bother and "oh
the molding and drips" they complain.

If painted correctly, no one notices the care and
attention paid to detail. The finished room looks so
clean, complete, no snags of the eye.

I enjoy the solitude of painting. Working on a canvas of
limited yet boundless scope. Never rush for good
results:
Prep, patch, sand, tape, paint, second coat (?), all done
in elastic time. The "Jackson Pollack like" aged drop
cloth below collecting new unwanted additions.

When painting, I like to close off the outside world and
work in silence losing track of time. The four walls
become a circumscribed universe. This therapeutic
endeavor of routine repeated physical acts allows the
mind to wander, relax and hum at a low modulation.

Buried memories resurface that no number of coats can
adequately cover. I could give you such a memory but
why side track or interrupt this meditation? Some
memories are not for sharing, you have enough of your
own.

We painters form a communal link to the former and future painters of a room. Some leave unintended brush strokes that denote past presence as my unintended signature clues will live on for a period of time.

Japanese ceramics purposely leave a flaw as an homage to nature, not necessary here, as there are plenty of my own mistakes if you look closely enough. But the overall finished project is a worthwhile upgrade I take much pride in.

My room painting days are numbered now
Oh how I will miss the challenge to make a beautiful smooth clean future of any color I desire using just my labor and will!
That's a skill we never wish to relinquish.

Hey, "do you think the bedroom could use a little refreshing before I start to wash these brushes and fold up the drop cloth?"

The Stage Is Set

December family holiday party, food prepared, table
set, gifts wrapped, wine chosen, the house is quiet,
anticipation palpable

Son calls offering to pick up bread
Brother calls to say nephew can make it
I, the default patriarch today, have smiling ghosts
hovering nearby

Perhaps this is the best moment
Anticipation trumping reality
Each hungry guest rehearsing a desired expectation,
noise, laughter, smiles, crumpled wrapping paper,
clattering silverware, clinking glasses, and chocolate
smudged napkins to follow

We know who will vie for attention, who will recede
Roles parceled out long ago
Some subjects verboten,
there will be trespassers
Red lines will gingerly be crossed

Children grow, fabric gets stretched
Wisdom and invisible control slowly slide down the
table to those once relegated to the children's section

All is as it should be
A happy time will be had by all
A glow will slowly diminish until reignited next year

The house will soon be empty
My wife and I will wearily clean up
And with gratitude the welcomed silence
That befalls us, grows a bit louder each year

Writers Block

I know some things

Hispanic laborers laying pavers,
should wear gloves, knee pads and masks

It's futile to wait for generosity from others
It's either there or it isn't

Some people buy eighty dollar tee shirts
while wearing cheap watches
Relationships to money are like individual fingerprints

Treat people like dogs
first show them the back of your open hand
then watch their tails or teeth

People are people
to expect otherwise is to be disappointed
but how to give up the expectations?

A blank page can be a treasured gift or
a herculean task for another day
the mind untethered

I don't know so many things

The weather vane spins in the wind
no direction home today

The Land of Humans

My son calls on the phone,
my wife, seems way too eager to please.
My son comes over, I am way too eager to please.
The land of hypocrisy is an overpopulated continent.

I still get anxious before social gatherings.
They always go well, time after time.
The inability to profit from experience
is to live in the land of the common people.

To think our thoughts have some universality
is to live in the land of the continually surprised.
To think tomorrow will be just like today
is to live in the land of naïve.

And we survive
Stepping in the same mud puddles over and over.
And we find new ones all the time
in the not so simple land of humans.

The Garden

In your teens and early twenties, or perhaps for as long as you have, you wander through the garden looking for the hidden roses among the weeds. You touch stems and sniff fragrances growing wildly here and there, the cornucopia of undefined desires, repugnancies and indifferences.

Perhaps the yellow flowers are inhaled as best friends. The blue violets you smell, but do not touch. Some you're drawn closer to, and perhaps their thorns draw unintended blood. One or two you snip with sharp shears when the blossom does not come, or fades too quickly.

You become a lifetime florist collecting bouquets of flowers over and over, replacing dying wilted ones with fresh vibrant colors anew. You think you can distinguish the annuals from the perennials, but time shows this to be a tricky game.

Does your aging discerning eye notice the nuance of shades you once were blind to? Are the true red roses, the ones that definitely draw intended blood, and are they the only beautiful ones you love forever despite the pain?

New Jersey Heat Wave 2023

Went for a boat ride around marsh lands on the Hackensack River near the Meadowlands. Our guide pointed out egrets and a bald eagle nest. He explained the tides and the grasses and other wild life.

We were bordered by roadways and a turnpike. Commuter trains passed back and forth over multiple bridges. There were some birds' nests cradled in the underneath rusted girders. Planes flew overhead to three nearby airports. As if on a string, every half mile another plane queued up in a landing pattern.

I was struck by the abutment of man and technology against shrinking nature. Modernity and progress surrounding protected marshes, each making begrudging accommodations for the other.

The hubris to take, transform and diminish old wetland ecosystems that existed eons before man, to distort and pollute, in the unyielding wave of science and progress.

The sole goal to go faster and further than ever before, belies some sacred respect for evolution of the natural planet that gets shunted aside in the name of advancement. There are repercussions modern science and technology has yet too fully comprehend.

The march to dominate nature with asphalt, steel and concrete comes with a cost to be reckoned with, as self cannibalization in the name of progress has a tipping point we are shaking hands with today.

Onion Skin or Pruning Season

Philip Roth advised "write as if you're dead."
Truman Capote did, and sabotaged, humiliated and
angered his "friends."

Sixty-nine years of scanning the landscape has
led me to disappointment.
I do not have the combination to open the vault.
I bring my tools, insignificant as they are.
I cannot crack the code.
I do not speak the language or languages.

Do I miss the clues; misread the smiles, the sighs and
the laughter?
Can I learn a different way that's foreign to my instinct?
Do I want to?
I'm tired but still yearning, the hunger always returns.

Waves crashing the shore smooth the jagged rocks
I do not have their eons of time.

Overcoming youthful shyness with glacial patience
while the clock's momentum seems to accelerate
as I extend my hand, speak my dialect, barter my wares
and bestow my gifts.

Only to confront indifferent faces or self-absorbed souls
that try to carry me along their riptide leading to
gnarled balls of seaweed or just out to sea.

I will not attempt to tease you the reader, so hear me:

Parties A&B, could not muster the will to respond when
receiving unsolicited personal gifts I mailed to their
homes.

Parties C & D ignored our invitation and excluded us
from their get together.

Parties D & E could not reach out or even acknowledge
the death of a dear relative?

Alas, a measured response was meted out with selective
demeanor, or silence was chosen, as a gift is a gift.
The length and depth of "questioned friendship" must
be taken into account in handling such delicate affairs.

I know what I know.
I adjust, conform, compromise, and smudge the line.
Yet I never, never, ever, ever question what I know to
be pure gold.

I believe there are many pilgrims along the road testing
their fellow strangers with a multitude of strategies
each on the same parallel quest seeking a common code
as they weigh their onion skin or wonder if it's pruning
season?

The Hurt Poem

People show so little respect
When they fail to act as we expect

The cost of business in this life
Suck it up and just accept the strife?

I'd give you my place in line
And you wouldn't even give me the time

But when expectations fail
Do we confront our transgressors and begin to wail?

You didn't even call when my brother died
You acted as if it were one big lie

Keep quiet don't let on and silently seethe,
how assertive should one be?

Stand tall and don't hold a grudge
Or defend your ego refusing to budge?

I write to ask for your review
And you fail to reply as if it's your due

You make me question my choices
As perhaps l tried to harmonize with all the wrong
voices

Of course you say, it depends on the relationship
Those we cherish and those we flip

The hurt remains as well as my distain
And I profit from this experience
As I let you fade into the distance

I thought we were friends, but I misread your language
of it depends

I thought we were friends, but I misread your smile that
was really a denial

I was willing to risk more and for you it felt like a chore

Take your leave like a cast away stone and let me grieve
here on paper, all alone

Moods

The weather changes
the sun shines anew
winds diminish, temperatures regulate
optimism reemerges
fever breaks
normalcy returns
the human appetite rebounds
and pain abates
the immediacy of major issues
can recede into the background
with comet like speed
the real catalyst can remain unknown
Yesterday's dilemma of hopeless
existential angst— of which is worse?
"Never finding a savior after decades of searching
or realizing there is no savior or never was"
no longer tethers its rope to the huge
helium balloon jettisoning away,
removing the giant overhead shadow
The Buddhist belief - that this life is to suffer
and we can only know suffering if we
have some contentment, calm, pleasure
we search for cause and effect
immersion and expulsion as if
rationality rules
but like the tides and the winds
we are passive slaves to moods
beyond our griping the reins of the
now tranquil stallions, that follow some
hopeful trail, until spooked again
we have no choice or perhaps, the best
remedy, is just the imperfect human
struggle to accept what is

Musing Death

Death is the ultimate reality teacher.
It calls your bluff on finagling and deal making.
It takes away your bargaining chip of time.
It's the real deal, the big stick, the Sultan of Swat.
Your toughest opponent, the master you can never beat.

Denial gives you the illusion of winning for a time.
Your life is the excitement and thrill of seeming to win,
but don't look over your shoulder or get to far ahead or
you'll see the game is rigged.
How difficult it is to really learn this lesson.

Western thinkers say death is either cessation of
sensation or an ascent to the divine. Neither a cause for
worry (?) Eastern religions of Hinduism and Buddhism
believe that one's status in the afterlife is a reward or
punishment for their conduct during this life.

We are free to pick our name, our religion and our
beliefs about death. Who said "We audition attitudes
regarding death like distinct bitter herbs on our
palate?"

Shakespeare said,
"Comfort is in heaven, we live on earth."
John Lennon said,
"Whatever gets you through the night."
You didn't really expect me to say anything better than
that, did you?

A Race?

It's a race, between knowing all the answers and dying.
Which will come first? By knowing, I mean figuring it
all out, a unified theory of life, where all the pieces fit, a
completed puzzle.

I'm getting closer every day, I can feel it. I wonder if
you get a cheat sheet right before you die.
You know, the answers are all revealed like looking in
the back of the book. Or rather is it like reading a novel
where you never get to the last chapter?

We are driven to accumulate knowledge or wisdom,
if you like, in great insatiable gulps.
The body might be declining but the mind is always
hungry to experience, absorb and integrate.

I know I won't live to be three hundred. So, I'm
traveling as swiftly as possible seeking satisfying
comprehension as I race death to the finish line.

A Mutiny

I have a 70 year old prostate, does it know that?
O yea it does, it doesn't sleep so well these nights and
it's kind of cranky. It's growing larger like its nearby
cousin, my belly, and they have co-opted my ears and
nose as well. My forehead got the message and my hair
keeps getting lost.
There's a mutiny going on here!

Longer naps and shorter short-term memories. Did we
drop anchor? Why did I come in my cabin again?
I can't find my maps anywhere.

My wisdom has grown larger as my audience has
grown smaller. My standing has grown while my
stature has shrunk. Three legged stool softeners are the
comfort of choice on this ship.
There's a mutiny going on here!

I inadvertently sat down on a closed toilet seat late last
night. Nature had called, attention wasn't paid, what a
surprise I got! There's a mutiny going on here!

Starting to read better without my glasses!
And what's your name again, matey?
It's right on the tip of my losing taste buds tongue.
Oh, I know there's a mutiny going on here alright.

We spar, we grapple, and we fence with an invisible
undefeated mutineer. All to keep the adventurous heart
at sea. Longing for one more voyage before landing on
an unearthly shore. Touché en garde.

As we begrudgingly continue to walk the plank
together and we ain't going to Tahiti?

Vulnerability

The gray tidal wave is coming for my generation;
sweeping asunder the best, the worst, and the average.
The tides ebb and flow since before we arrived, we
watch and count the swells. Keep your eyes straight
ahead; to glance to the side is to witness the carnage.

You have a medical issue.
You make an appointment.
The doctor runs some tests.
The results arrive.
The doctor advises you to see his colleague.
The fear, the panic, the "what ifs."
One sentence, "I think you should see a specialist."

Your life changed irrevocably, you yearn for yesterday
Your shadowy path darkened in a forest you just
entered and may never exit.

The specialist calms your fears, "We can do this, it's
manageable, let's not get ahead of ourselves."
There's sunlight now streaming into your forest.
You joyfully re-enter your placid world of yesterday
humbled, appreciative, you have escaped for the time
being.

What have you really learned?
The randomness, the luck, the vulnerability
to experience the forest in sunlight and shadow
just connects us to all those that came before.
Is that enough?

Linguists

We are all linguists albeit poor ones as we try and crack the codes of the languages spoken all around us.

We engage or observe in the hopes of deciphering the unspoken messages inundating us all the time. Some hit and some miss their targets when we interact with say, a different economic group, a foreigner, a doctor, a hardware store owner or bank teller.

We listen, process and search for clues, friend or foe, helpful or obstinate, talking down or kissing up, letting us in, walling us out, bridging, venting, praising, dominating, camouflaging, reassuring, testing etc. etc. etc. etc. etc. There's usually another underlying message we try and tap into rather than just the surface content.

Every family has their own style and language. Observe and listen to new in-laws exchanging pleasantries with the intact family. Every spouse, boyfriend, girlfriend, co-worker, etc. uses vocabulary with intent, style, spacing, timing, innuendo, rhythm, to probe, distance, communicate, etc.

"Your haircut looks great"
"I feel for you"
"You can't trust them"
"Will you just do this for me?"
"You're my best friend"
"I hate you"
"I love you"

How different the written language from the audio, from the face-to- face. So much to process- words, style, tone, body language all in a nanosecond. They say we think three times faster than we speak, giving us time to factor in our triggers, history, accuracy, perception, mood, etc.

We are not blank slate blackboards, being overlaid with fresh chalk, but a cornucopia percolating in an underground cauldron distinctly unique and separate from the speaker you're listening to. It's a wonder you can read and understand this attempt to talk to you in my language.

What do you hear?

Metamorphosis

Saw a famous well respected PhD author on television
this morning, pontificating in earnest with humor and
intelligence about religion, society, economics and
government policies.

The author was an older person who in his lifetime had
changed, among other things, his sex, his religion and
his political belief system. It's good to grow, evolve and
process new experiences. Is that not learning from life
and maturing?

Our views are not carved in stone at thirty. They're
fluid, or so we think. Yet, this author's views and life,
had shifted so starkly one could ask, "why believe
anything he was telling us today?"

As next month, next year, these views might not hold.
Where is the center, truth, if core beliefs can shift so
radically? Are we wasting our time or just frolicking
earnestly when speaking to each other, are we deluding
ourselves thinking this time, "we got it."

Or do we accept our limitations, hypocrisies and
transformations as the inevitable cost of living?
How thin the ground we tread,
forgetting the molten core below.

Where Are We Headed?

I start walking fast, then running in an open field.
The shelling gets louder and closer. I begin sprinting as
shells begin to explode so close that black earth stings
my face. My panic turns to the realization I cannot
outrun certain death. I will die here. As I freeze, fate
intervenes, silence, the barrage has suddenly stopped.

I make my way to an underground subway station.
It's packed with silent citizens huddled together with
the illusion of safety. Should I stay or should I leave?
I venture out on to the bombed out panic stricken
streets.

A tattered bus approaches, recklessly maneuvering
around debris and huge pot holes. The stench of
charred bodies and burning buildings engulfs the
nostrils. I climb on board with several other dead eyed,
shock, grieved passengers.

There's a middle aged woman ranting, "I have papers.
The party won't hurt me. My sister's not so lucky.
Mother should have listened to me."

There are no empty seats. I scan the other passengers
who are speaking in hushed tones.
I wonder who has money strapped to their ankles.
I wonder who has food hidden under their shirts.
I wonder who will lie about their neighbor.

I look at the ashen driver, slumped low in his seat. He
has a bandaged hand, thick forearms, is ashen, with
steely eyes focused straight ahead. He wears a religious
symbol on a tarnished chain that he unconsciously
keeps touching.

Didn't he used to work in the town market with his
wife? Where is she?

We leave the city limits.
Where are we going?
How long will it take?
Will we get there safely?

Is this Europe?
Is this Asia?
Is this America?
Does it matter?

For me it's a bad dream
For others it's a nightmare reality
The world keeps witnessing
Time immemorial

Nothing New You Say

Sunday, we went to see a foreign film. Coming home
we passed an angry man loudly ranting at the sky.
On the same avenue we passed a homeless woman
lying horizontally on a bench wearing filthy clothes and
loudly beseeching us for money.

Monday night, at our meditation session, near the
church entrance a young homeless girl wrapped in a
blanket hunkered down for the evening, just out of the
rain. She ate cookies while we meditatively walked
around a mandala inside, safely protected from the
weather.

Tuesday night our 35th wedding anniversary my wife
and I celebrated at a very expensive restaurant. We
drink plenty of Pinot Noir and finished with fancy
desserts. Most waiters and staff were brown skinned
and came from another continent. We learned business
was good 350 seatings were expected that night.

Friday, we will service over 350 families with fresh
produce at the food pantry some waiting in line for
over two hours.

The polarization of the American Dream
never more evident, many empty storefronts
and crowded coffee shops selling five dollar lattes.

Flights to Paris are overbooked this year, while
Chapter 11 filings are higher than they've been in a
decade.

Friends of ours decide not to go to Portland Maine due to homeless situation as police plan to clear a growing tent encampment.

We read poetry to each other as fires originating hundreds of miles away foul our air. How, with equanimity, do we square the equation placed right before our eyes in the America of 2023?

The feeble response of "It's always been this way" only worsens the cracks in the thawing pond of America as if acceptance is the normal reaction to do nothing.

Thoughts Walking in the Woods

The meditative mind of a long distance traveled
ignited by a contemplative walk in the forest
Should I remove my shoes to receive the earth's energy?

Selecting random memory files from the cabinet
Remembering to remember when:

As a child I grasped my mother's hand when crossing
the street together

The thrill of unsteadiness on the first bike ride when my
father let go of the rear fender, and I didn't fall

Hearing my unborn son's heart beat in my wife's womb
Taking my young son's hand when we crossed the
street together

The thrill I felt when the pretty dark haired girl let me
remove her blouse

Renting my first apartment with the kitchen sink down
the hall

Making love to a woman who would later become my
wife in a dark Paris hotel room during a summer
lightning storm

Three times saying a final goodbye to my mother
as her body lay still as a mountain at dawn

The temporal experience is as invisible as oxygen itself
Where do these memories reside when we depart?
Does it jettison into the universal library of the cosmos?

Ah, and when this contemplative walk is over,
The value you ask?
I do not presume an answer

I just hope to one day hold the hand of my future grandchild and when we cross the street together; I hope they feel the safe bond of connection.

To Bridge the Divide

June is when the honeysuckle flowers bloom
when a sweet flowery perfume pleasantly, invisibly
provokes your awareness in a delightful way

If I try to think of the smell when the flower is not
present, my nostrils flare, I involuntarily inhale, and
some imperfect semblance of the actual fragrance comes
to mind

Each time I wade or plunge into water, it's as if the first
time, the weightlessness, the buoyancy the thrill, maybe
an ancient memory of the universally experienced
amniotic pool? The difference between the memory of
sensation and the actual experience is but a thin real
membrane of separation

But love transcends these feelings and memories
It exists in the present, the tangible and equally well in
the mind whether to touch or just think of loved ones
I love the smell of honeysuckle, the immersion into
water, but love retains its perfection by linking past and
present indelibly in a special way never to cleave

Perspective

October sun has slipped behind the clouds
there's a chill in the air
I zip my ten-year-old jacket up tight

A friend's husband had collapsed in the shower
taken to the hospital
two days of tests and observations
he was released yesterday

Last night in bed
my friend turned
to her husband
to find he was dead

Recently at a hospital
I filled out all the forms,
put on a gown,
and watched the nurse insert an IV

Then wheeled into a bright room
and waited for the doctor
while the anesthesiologist tapped away on his phone
and nurses chattered in background

I tried to relax
taking slow deliberate breathes,
watching the second hand on the wall clock
acknowledging my surrender

Doctor finally arrived, smiled and the
anesthesiologist said "have a nice sleep"
Entered wonderful limbo state
I could stay forever on this nether bridge,
I wonder if this is just death's preview

Confusion

Walked into a fancy men's store
Bought a seventy dollar colored tee shirt
Made of "Tensil" and has an animal logo on the back
Looks just like my other fifteen dollar colored tee shirts
that are neatly folded away in a nicked-up veneered
chest

Not sure why I bought it
Wanted to see how I would feel?
Grateful I could splurge,
chagrined that I overpaid
A lost game of chicken with the sales clerk

I wear a cheap Timex watch
My car is ten years old
There are homeless a few miles from here
No one notices or comments on my new tee shirt
at the town pool

Birthday Anxiety

Did I mention I'm thinking of taking a course in Wise Aging?

Did I mention that I misplace names, words, titles and facts like forgotten items put on a top shelf in a dark closet, and later, when no longer needed, are surprisingly rediscovered?

Did I mention it's on my fingertips, it's on the tip of my tongue, and it ain't there when I need it?

Did I mention aches no longer recede like the tides, they linger like the moon?

Did I mention prostate and cataracts ripening on the vine that will soon need tending?

Did I mention ejaculations that once danced like the Tango, now, if lucky feel like toothpaste squeezed from a tube?

Did I mention doors closing, nailed shut forever?

Did I mention titillation is now a memory past?

The eyes and mind feast on banquets already eaten, yet the hunger remains.

Did I mention these are the golden years?
Family, friends, acquaintances exiting the stage, subtracted from the equation, moving on, death the great equalizer, pick your trite euphemism?

Birthdays to be celebrated, really?

112

Did I mention I humbly acknowledge, so far I've been very lucky overall, as things go?

Yet I can't help but comment on the changing landscape, monitoring this slippage whether we tune in or tune out.

Did I mention that we complain to those that listen?

Did I mention that we complain to those that don't?

Did I mention we are, as far as I can tell, no different from those who came before us?

Did I mention we live in the best of all times which makes little difference unless you weigh time as gold?

Did I mention I'm thinking of taking a course in Wise Aging?

Did I mention it's my birthday this week?

Questions

Buried our mother two years ago
Father gone decades before
Gray hairs are sprouting in my eyebrows
Of an age when no longer improving
More time to worry about the world
Old friends scatter or sheared
Replacements mere replicas and inferior configurations
The core mind strong and desirous,
the fringe starting to wear and fray

Life's roadmaps mostly traveled, its souvenirs
collecting dust. The sign posts and directions ahead are
vague and amorphous, which path to follow now, those
of tried and true conventions, or the idiosyncratic exotic
off road lonelier deviations?

Which path to happiness, or is that the wrong question?
Struggling for the right questions with a tasting menu
of options like mirages evaporating before us
As we are dragged or sprint toward oblivion

Stroll by the Beach

On a summer day more than thirty years ago, my wife and I strolled along Beach Avenue near the ocean and dunes in Cape May New Jersey. We were taking the long walk from our motel into town for lunch.

We side-stepped the elderly couples who moved too slowly for our liking. You know the paunchy, baseball capped, white haired or balding men, some with hearing aids and their overweight wives in baggy shorts displaying blue veined mottled thighs and wearing floral tops and oversized hats.

We didn't give these couples a passing thought; they were but a slight inconvenience on this fine sunny day with a hint of salt in the breeze. Now with the wisdom that only arrives with time I hope my wife and I will someday be an elderly couple walking slowly near the beach.

Funny, how age locks us into such a narrow vision. How our sense of self, limits us to the panorama of possibilities. How much have we missed or misunderstood because of the "I"?

In the not so distant future will my wife and I understand the younger couples whose path we unintentionally impede?

It's easier to understand looking backward. Can we trust our vision to see all that there is, or was, or will be?

The Human Condition

I go to the barber but he can't help my thinning hair
and enlarging balding pate.
But he trims as best he can and recommends a good
Italian restaurant.

I go to the dentist but he can't regrow my teeth or save
my receding gums.
But he fills my cavities and recommends toothpaste and
a good movie.

I go to the orthopedist but she can't reverse my arthritis
or shrinking skeleton.
But she recommends exercises, a comfortable shoe and
offers a stock tip.

I go to the cemetery and only recall memories.
There are no recommendations here.
Death, like quantum mechanics, is something we accept
but don't understand.

Life is generally good. It's wide and deep and I try to
accept the bumps in the winding road.
Mondays, Wednesdays, Fridays and Saturdays I'm
copasetic with all the above.

Tuesdays, Thursdays and Sundays are another matter.
On these days I lament, moan and complain about the
human condition to a silent universe.

Glaucoma is robbing my vision, colitis is rotting my
intestines, and my arteries are narrowing like my
possibilities. I sadly see my generation afflicted,
slowing, aging, on the brink of disappearing.

We have replaced our elders with no greater wisdom. From which book shall I now read, from whom shall I now listen, who knows the truth?

On Mondays, Wednesdays, Fridays and Saturdays I deny my fate and joyfully play in "the garden of delight." I still feel young, hopeful and optimistic. I still feel that love, success, adulation, prosperity are within my reach. I believe things will stay good forever; death is for others not coming to my doorstep.

Tuesdays. Thursdays and Sundays I look in the mirror and ask how did this happen? Where did my father's face come from? I feel dispirited, resigned and gloomy. I envy the youth that has forsaken me. I hear bad news from specialists who take my serenity and smash it to pieces. I know the future portends a downhill slide for which no brakes exist. I feel little is possible, the door is closing, the sunlight shrinking.

The calendar keeps rolling over, Mondays to Tuesdays to Wednesdays and on and on. Each day no stronger than the next. The only winning is to accept and reconcile what each day brings.

Forever

When we shut off the radio, the music stops,
but the vibrations continue unheard by us, forever

When we shut off the light, the rays continue, unseen
by us, speeding away, forever

What happens to all the "I love you's" spoken and felt?
Where do those feelings go, forever?

Are they retained only in memory?
No, they're out there with the music and light
instilling life in the dark universe, forever

To the Critics

My fellow poets want me to write simple intelligent
photographic descriptive poems of, red wheel barrows,
high fences, or golden withered autumn leaves

They say use no clichés, no improper grammar or
punctuation, no run- on sentences or misspellings that
might garner poetic point deductions

My voice sings a different tune
Not unlike another old Brooklyn boy named Whitman
My scribbling's lack rhyme, strict meter, natural
cadence, and have extended lines
Neat three or four line stanzas occur per chance not by
design
My improper road less traveled offends the erudite
tailored tuxedos of poetic galas
And slums with the second rate education of the
undiscovered

Oh let us praise the personal explorers roaming the
plains of non-understanding, with their unlimited
questions but not unlimited time, about self-nature and
the universe

Hey, make some elbow room with your decrees, not
your tribal restrictions barring the door, hands capping
your ears and scowls stretched tight across the literary
elite

Your yacht today, perhaps assaulted by multitudes of
dinghies, does not rule the shining sea from shore to
shore, as the riptides of poetry are constantly changing
"Steer for the deep waters"

Who are we playing to?
What crowd, audience are we slavishly devoting our
constant audition energy?
As if we're counting, courting votes from a world of
apathetic nonvoters
What's our spiel, which wares are we selling?
We deliver our well-rehearsed lines in print,
 faces and voices absent
Like fisherman trolling, chumming the sea
we hope to snag fish by their tails or fins or better yet to
hook them whole

Maybe they escape or we release them, returning to the
ocean battered, affected or oblivious, seeking out the
next tempting line no longer interested in our lure or
barb

Just sing, sing your own song with the one voice you
have, that's enough

Game On

So this how the game is played.

The clock is set silently ticking.
You start with willful ignorance.
Add some detachment, then if you're lucky, twenty or
thirty symptom free years to form an air of invincibility.

Perhaps the first real harbinger is the death of a
grandparent. Then you might notice some creaky knees
or maybe a slightly stiff back. Then perhaps a friend or
acquaintance leaves the scene prematurely.

Then maybe a little high blood pressure, a murmur or a
cholesterol level the doc doesn't like. Your hearing,
eyesight and taste decline so slowly you hardly notice.
Who needs all their teeth or hair anyway?

Some pills and procedures for this and that, and the
game continues. Sprinkle in some vitamins, more
vaccinations and doctors' appointments and the game
goes another round.

You try and gather your courage, as your opponent just
sits smiling and nodding at you. Like an unbalanced
seesaw your physical rigor declines as your emotional
troubles go skyward.

Maybe a sibling, or a parent or two departs, as you
climb the ladder and survey the scene from on high.

A small lump, a shadow, or maybe a sore that doesn't heal, spin the wheel, pick a number or watch the dice tumble.

Death doesn't worry, death doesn't sweat it.
Death play's the long game.
The house always wins.

You know that, you just didn't think "you" were playing for keeps. One by one the cards from the hand of denial are being plucked away.

Lose good sex, lose good food, lose mobility,
You lose, lose, lose.

You're in the big leagues now.
But the real message of the game that takes so long to learn, is just how precious time is.

And the old cliché you were told, is as valid as ever.
"It's not about winning or losing but ...."

Landscape at Seventy

By age seventy you gain a mental acuity looking
backward and forward as never before.

You're in prison and liberated at the same time. You
can't escape, but brilliant sunlight shines through the
bars. You lose youthful inhibitions gaining wisdom,
insight and restraint.

You used to think you were a fast walker, not so true
when you walk with a younger person these days.
Deciding not to sprint a hundred yards for a bus is not a
tough decision anymore. You think you can flirt, only to
confront your foolishness if put to the test.

When younger you avoided the old slow white haired
cashier at aisle four, now you have compassion for her
having to work at this stage in life and offer to buy her a
cup of coffee.

The world can be an inner delight. A simple walk in the
botanical gardens with your wife, a radio song that
moves you to tears, an inner peace that settles like silent
falling snow.

An inner happiness expands as you watch a friend play
and sing in a septuagenarian band. You tap your foot
and nod your head to an old Duke Ellington tune.

Enjoying both Gillespie and Springsteen, not a narrow one way street anymore but a vast complex highway that youth had previously prevented an entrance ramp to. You respect and admire these seventy year olds playing with competency and determination trying their best without magical illusions of grandeur.

You're able to view the world more as it is without the blinders and petty biases of younger days. The inside blurriness of confusion recedes while outside physicality declines. To be seventy is to be tethered to the world while viewing it from a mile high.

This was the great plan, the deal, the Yin and the Yang as they say. You weren't asked to play or bargain. You were just given a seat at the table for a random hand to be dealt and to just appreciate and decipher all the inside and the outside landscape with awe and astonishment.

It's Simple

Last week, I watched a movie about Stalin starving millions in the Ukraine.

I'm currently reading a book about the American dust bowl of the 1930s.

Yesterday, driving in upstate NY I drove past apple orchards where you pick your own apples for $34.50 per half bushel.

Coming home, buying lunch in a diner I paid $25 for a hamburger, fries and apple pie.
Inflation is eating America.

Today, I manned my station at the food pantry.
I loaded apples, sweet potatoes, watermelons, boxes of produce and a limited supply of (soon to be outdated) pies and pastries into a several hundred cars.
I save the pies and pastries for the older dilapidated cars, the ones with disabled placards hanging from their rear view mirrors, or cars that have young children sitting in them.
You should see the smiles when you place an oversized green striped bowling ball of a melon onto a young kids lap.
A whole car says "thank you" and "God bless you" when you pass a large apple pie through a driver's side window.

Today a smiling older man drove up in a new foreign convertible sports car with the roof down.
He wore gold jewelry and a bright red baseball cap with a designer logo on it.
I didn't offer him any pies or pastries.

I wanted to ask questions, why are you here, what's
your story, are you aware of the perception?
My thoughts belied my actions. I silently loaded his car
with the allotted produce.
It is not proper to ask such questions.
The other Buddhist volunteers thanked him for coming
and wished him a great weekend.
He drove off, closing the roof of his car.

Sometimes it's better not thinking about history,
governments, taxes, serendipity, the wealth gap,
stations in life, and what is fair,
it's best to just volunteer
to give food to people
who say they are
hungry.

Maintenance

Morning
alarm rings,
rise, shower brush teeth
eat breakfast

Do laundry, pay electric bill
renew magazine subscription
get car inspected

Afternoon
doctor's appointment
biopsy, wait, bad results

Next week,
surgery, until clear borders
stitches ooze, wound care,
mind scab forms
schedule follow up appointments

Six months later,
more biopsies,
special diet, pills, prayers
more procedures
grim faces
piece by piece subtracted
a jigsaw puzzle coming undone

One year later
Perpetual routinized maintenance
as the seasons change
but not vigilance

According to Plan

I like to stroll in the town's Olmstead designed park.
Usually, two laps around the circular black asphalt path
is fine. Walking among the trees and open rolling green
fields clears my mind.

I came upon a young father, of medium height, trim,
bearded, wearing a black tee shirt and gray shorts. He
lifted his young son, clad in black pants, a blue shirt,
and small white sneakers, out of a stroller.

Father and son held hands as the boy took some wobbly
steps. After a few yards, the boy released hands and
unsuccessfully wandered ahead before falling to the
ground. Startled and slightly scared the toddler
awkwardly managed to stand.

He looked backward, instinctively making eye contact
with his father and grasped the steadying older hand.
After a few yards walking in this manner, the boy again
let go, reclaiming his independence.

As I passed them again on my second lap. I saw the
little boy was now far ahead of his father.
I said to the father, "he's getting braver."
The father smiled and nodded.

Heading home I thought how often this simple pattern
of behavior is repeated throughout life if things go
according to plan.

The Hand We Play

I know a woman handcuffed to her life
caretaker to both a disabled husband and grown son
forced to work and push wheelchairs
as the weight of circumstance tries to drown her soul

I know a man restricted by anxiety who cannot
physically visit the places his mind travels to
The dichotomy of thought and action
the prison of phobia

I know an older person who's lost his desire for any
change, novelty and seeks boredom and routine as
if this suit of armor will safely protect him

The struggle, the price to be paid
to battle these so human conditions
seems to inflate the older we get,
yet to not struggle is the price to exist
without living

I see those who try to escape
through the accumulation of knowledge or wealth
or pass the time as musicians, lovers
or perhaps distracted by religion,
to fill the time metered out by nature

Is it best to think of such things,
or better to choose to be immersed in anything
and be oblivious and self-absorbed in the carnival of life
before the coming of the final silence?

Candidly Speaking

"It's good and bad" she said.
"What do you mean" I asked?"
"At my age I could walk into a room naked and no one
would notice."

She continued, "The playing field has been leveled
my words are taken more at face value now rather than
some unspoken code that might be misinterpreted.
The sexual tension has been replaced by placid
indifference."

She continued "The art of flirtation has been put away
in a drawer."
She made a joke, "it's like you're playing poker with a
deck of only deuces. Flirtation's charm would be
replaced by embarrassment or at least
inappropriateness if tried today."
She stated this with a smile as well as with some
resignation as both emotions simultaneously spread
across her face.

"Makeup, crow's feet, graying hair, a white eyebrow or
two forgotten to be plucked, just the costume nature
provides for the changing role," she lamented.
"Time to dwell inward or see the reality of the world
in a new light free of the male gaze."
That role played for so long on all stages
whether wanted or unwanted.

Continuing our conversation she said
"Freedom, but freedom at a great cost"
touching my arm to emphasize the point.
"I once had more attention than I wanted
Now I have less attention than I need."

Saying goodbye we briefly hugged.
I felt her breast press against my chest.
She lingered an extra beat,
then showed me out,
so that she could accept the night
with its immense dark sky and all its twinkling stars.

Ask the Lonely

No.
Everyman is an island of divergent strata
each person a different click
on a colossal combination lock

You foolishly think other people think as you do
want to go to the beach in the summer
strive for relevance in their lives
and note when a social injustice has occurred

You're often wrong
surprised by your error, and misjudgment
the vault stays locked despite attempting multiple
combinations

Accept this fate with equanimity
or struggle to debate, persuade, argue?

What is your default, your *motus operandi*
was it thought out, analyzed, adjusted by experience,
or did self-blindness, lead you to the safety of some
conformity?

We dismiss you, turn our backs to you,
We need you. we open our arms to embrace you

I'll let you contemplate your reply in solitude
while I go down to the sea, struggling to accept the
waters that separate us

May 15th

Four AM

Soft slight chilly breeze rustles the curtains, quiet
thoughts enter, cool sheets buffeted by stillness.

When you're a certain age, there's a good size row boat
of people who we once were close to. They have sailed
to distant shores lonely, hurt, we, I grieve their loss and
try to replace them. I misjudge these replacements
thinking they are manifestations of the missing.
Assuming things I shouldn't, confused when they fail to
act like my ghosts.

I wonder what apparition I look like in their memories?
Attempted to reach out to the living ghosts that made
up the past, we, I, cowardly wait for them to act first,
afraid to alter, revisit the granite of the past for who
knows what transformations I might encounter now.

I am a coward and write a poem instead. But poems are
just thoughts on paper not rowboats deciding which
direction to head.

Five AM

I stand in the cold dark hallway at five AM and for just
a moment feel the fear of being human. Some family,
friends' acquaintances already dead, stricken, dying
The herd being thinned by the lions. The shadows
creeping up the walls.

You, the doctor, who saved many and expanded the
sunlight with empathy and compassion, please answer
your phone, call me tell me you are alright.
I do not want your silence to be your final good bye.

I know an older woman who only prays when naked in
her bathroom. This is when she believes God is
listening. What currency can I trade for comfort?

All as It Should Be

We're hunkering down for the long haul
Getting a new roof and doing some home renovations
We had excitedly gone house hunting, sadly found
nothing we liked enough to justify a move

Chilly autumn arriving, in more ways than one
Reluctance and comfort, bookends on a shelf
Medical issues like poison mushrooms sprouting on the
lawn of friends and family
As our generation moves to the head of the line
No parents left to lean on
Children lack the wisdom we seek,
And are self-absorbed
All is as it should be
Yet doubts and fears and darkness little by little edge
out the sunlight
Knowing winter is not that far off

I watch my wife sip her coffee
I relish and fear the depth of our attachments,
The gravity of our bonds,
The narrow path only we walk alone,
Never before so clearly defined
All is as it should be
When I was young I respected my elders
I wanted them to tell me the secrets, the answers
They didn't
I am learning them now
All as it should be

I Know

I know a man who automatically assumes everyone he
meets is hurting more than him.

I know a woman who only prays when naked in her
bathroom.

I know a woman, who in social situations talks to the
loneliest person in the room in order to make them feel
more comfortable.

I know a woman who listens so well to others; she can't
hear her own screams.

I know people whose facial mask of aging is permanent
to all but a select loving few.

I know many who refuse to look into the mirror of life
as if it might be an angry jury.

I know a man who slices meat in a deli.
I asked him for a quarter pound of turkey.
"No cheese" he asked?
No I said "it's not healthy."
He replied, "You know, you should enjoy this life a
little."

Tethered by Memories

Every few years I feel the subterranean pull of
Brooklyn, one hour, 25 miles, 25 years and a lifetime
away. From suburban New Jersey I drive down Ocean
Parkway to former residences, memories flooding back
like a surgeon tapping parts of an exposed brain.

1980 Coyle Street's house looking so small and narrow,
now trace memories surface of the street not being fully
paved in 1955 and scary anti-Semitic Italian and Irish
boys living on the next block.

Ghosts materialize: Roger my first childhood friend, my
father and me having a baseball catch in the alley, my
parents calling the police when my older brother runs
away from home, getting only as far as Staten Island,
parents and older brother now deceased, birthdays,
graduations, Viet Nam, heart attacks, divorce, and the
families' unhappy version of "Our Town."

My first apartment at 1858 East 14th Street, the same
green door remains and the cement softball field is still
encircled by a high cyclone fence across the street. Just a
small third floor attic apartment for $115 a month with
cinderblock bookshelves, cable-spool table covered with
a batik print, and hanging beads as a room divider, just
the décor of the day; a place where "we practiced"
being married.

We moved in together at 2222 East 18th street, a six
story red brick apartment house where "our parent-
hood" blossomed. There my mother-in-law bathed our
newborn son in the kitchen sink, so gently cupping his
head, excitement and joy filling the room.

Several years later, feeling adult-like, we moved to a house 1842 Ryder Street, near pancake-flat Marine Park. The skylights that leaked are still there. The narrow pink house with the shared drive remains, but our Asian neighbors, Bill and Alice on one side and aged Mr. Wright, on the other side, who cut his lawn with scissors have long since departed.

I drive past elementary school PS 194, remembering all the punch ball games (of glory) in the schoolyard, cut short by a shrill teacher's whistle. Junior High PS 278 where "silent passing" was enforced in the hallways, where designated lines painted on the floor indicated where turns were permitted. If you forgot to wear a required tie, a funny bowtie was given to you as shameful punishment. Friday's at 3 pm felt like VE day, and Mrs. Zuckerman's red marks on my science papers could be forgotten till Monday.

I drive past Sheepshead Bay and Brighton Beach and Coney Island and on and on around my heartland. I wonder who are the people living in Brooklyn today?

I do not know them. Did I really know the other people a lifetime ago? The arc of a lifetime, constantly re-examined now from across the Hudson, tethered by memories conscious and unconscious, and embedded in my DNA. So now, when we speak, and you find me just a little different, remember that I am now a stranger of two lands.

Routines

Everything has a run
Everything comes to an end
You don't know this when you're young

Living in the moment precludes change
Not enough repetitions to know all things expire
Unconsciously expecting the run to continue forever

Be it a job
a friendship
a marriage
a weekly card game

Should we dwell, appreciate, think about the run in
progress or ride the wave, not looking sideways
until the forward motion ceases? Sometimes it ends
abruptly like an unexpected thunder clap, sometimes
gradually, like fingernail growth or melting snow

We know people die all the time
But somehow feel exempt,
quite the trick of self-deception

I think about the routines that map my life
the fragile patterns falsely thought to be so solid
and will continue to think about them long after this
meditation and still, hopefully continue writing poems

In Spite of Ourselves

Watched music clips for an hour this morning.
Lost my sense of time, absorbed by musicians
singers, songwriters; some of whom you may know
some maybe not, Jackson Browne, John Prine, Bob
Seeger, Willie Nelson, Levon Helm.

The clips jumped back and forth in time.
Young virile vibrant men contrasted with their older
selves, used up, time worn diminished stars of
yesterday.

In fact a few have already passed on.
The melancholy of witnessing youth dissolved
in minutes taps into a sadness impossible to ignore.
Old age is not a garment you just try on,
once fitted the season lasts forever
like the lyrics embedded in our mind.

We sing along to their youth, our youth, their loss, our
loss, their celebration our celebration.

And, our children cannot relate.
The stage remains constant; the players do not.
That's the plan.

Ready or Not
In Spite of Ourselves
Night Moves
Poncho and Lefty
The Night They Drove Old Dixie Down

A Sweet Evening

You and a friend unexpectedly invited us
to a Buddhist meditation session.
I replied without committing.
Surprise and a warm smile on your face
when you entered the monastery and saw us
sitting quietly, shoeless, waiting.

A black cat roamed the room
as a bald tattooed monk in robes
led us through forty five minutes of silence.

Afterward on a whim we invited you back
to our house and you welcomed the invitation.
You and your friend drank herbal tea,
my wife coffee and green tea for me.

Strangers of comparable age we connected
some of the parallel lines of our lives
in pleasant thoughtful conversation.

We hugged goodbyes.
I walked you to your car.

In early June in this part of the country
the sweet fragrance of honey suckle
can be found lingering in the air,
if we choose the right paths
either by chance or design.

A Friend Asked for a Poem about Death Today

It wasn't nature's prayers that brought us here.

At the food pantry I kibitz and joke with my fellow
volunteers as we laugh and try to gently outdo each
other in mock insult while serving the hungry with
hopeful gaiety and balanced reverence.

At the college philosophy class my seventy- two year
old male gaze marvels at the fresh young girlish faces
with their womanly bodies, that speak such wisdom.

At monthly gatherings that congregate at the town
library, we gently applaud fellow poets reading from
the lectern as they try to enthrall, connect and engage.

My emotions swell and deflate watching professional
athletes compete with utmost urgency over thrown,
caught and batted baseballs, as if life itself hangs in the
balance. Ah the joy of powerful emotions safely felt at a
distance with like-minded fans.

I walk with my wife in the Iris garden, marveling at the
variety and plethora of colors. I take her hand. I
photograph her for posterity attempting to freeze but a
precious moment in time. For whom you might ask?

We seek friends with patient ears that give thoughtful counsel to our heartfelt revelations and make us feel less singular.

A full weekend calendar of gatherings planned, cooking in, dining out, two outdoor parties, social conventions, sharing, and communion. Collect what we can, appreciate what we can, with deep gratitude; feeling the collective kiss on the cheek, and the human embrace of our brethren before Nature's executed plan, takes it all away from us.

That's my poem about death for today.

Bio

I'm writing a book
My editor wants some bio information
I mention my family, education, charity work, and
hiking

But I want to really reveal my struggle for equanimity
The lifetime search for balance between living
In the mind and living in the world
Observing and participating
Listening and talking
Seeking novelty and desiring routines
When to dive in, when to grip the railings
Introspection and extospection

Juggling with parity,
Positioning the
Awe and the mundane
Of this world,
Side by side
In proper perspective
That is my true living biography

Too contemplative, cerebral, general?
It's still a work in progress
Who's to say the book is ever completed?

Mark was born in Paterson, New Jersey, and moved to Brooklyn, New York at an early age. He holds a BA in Psychology from Richmond College CUNY, and a MS in Counseling from Long Island University. He is a proud member of The Brooklyn Bonnies Boys Club Baseball Hall of Fame. For the last twenty-five years, he has resided with his wife in Montclair and Cedar Grove New Jersey. His first book "Conversations with Myself" was published in 2017. Mark divides his time between family, community, and charity activities. He enjoys being a member of various discussion groups. His other interests include hiking, photography, exercising and exploring towns in and around New Jersey.

"My work is a blend of prose and poetry revealing the inner landscape of an individual without ignoring a much larger universality that we all experience." *Mark Shoenfield*